Granny PottyMouth's

FAST AS F*CK

COOKBOOK

Granny PottyMouth's
FAST AS F*CK
COOKBOOK

Tried-and-True Recipes
Seasoned With Sass

PEGGY GLENN

aka
Granny PottyMouth

PAGE STREET
PUBLISHING CO.

First published in 2018 by
Page Street Publishing Co.
27 Congress Street, Suite 105
Salem, MA 01970
www.pagestreetpublishing.com

Distributed by Macmillan, sales in Canada by The Canadian Manda Group.

22   21   20   19   18   1   2   3   4   5

ISBN-13: 978-1-62414-621-3
ISBN-10: 1-62414-621-X

Library of Congress Control Number: 2018932228

Cover and book design by Kylie Alexander for Page Street Publishing Co.
Photography by Erica Allen

Printed and bound in China

OH, MAN, I COULD GET IN SO MUCH TROUBLE FOR NOT DEDICATING THIS TO EVERY TEACHER, RELATIVE, FRIEND, LOVER AND MATE I'VE EVER HAD. BUT, AT MY AGE, I'M IN CHARGE, SO THEY CAN SUCK . . . UM . . . WHATEVER.

CUZ, IN TRUTH, I MUST DEDICATE THIS TO YOU—THE READER WHO SPENT YOUR HARD-EARNED BUCKS—WHO THINKS THIS SWEET-ASS BOOK OF RECIPES AND TIPS IS THE ANSWER TO ALL YOUR COOKING AND MEAL-PREP PROBLEMS. FRANKLY, IT IS, IF YOU READ IT AND DO THE SHIT I TELL YOU TO DO. I WROTE THIS FOR YOU, MY SWEET FUCKERS. ENJOY IT. THE RECIPES WILL MAKE YOU, AND ANYBODY WHO EATS YOUR CREATIONS, SCREECH "THIS IS MEGATITS!" IN ORGASMIC DELIGHT. AND, BE SURE TO WATCH MY FUNNY CRAP ON THE INNERTUBE AND THE BOOK OF FACE, TOO. DON'T EVER FORGET ME. I'LL KNOW IT IF YOU DO. GRANNY KNOWS! JUST ASK MY GRANDSONS AND MY DUDE!

CONTENTS

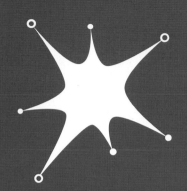

INTRODUCTION

I'm a legit granny—my grandsons are grown men, matter of fact. I learned to cook from two of the most brilliant women who ever lived: my dad's mom and my own mom. They made do with little and made it taste like shit you'd feed the rich people. I've been a military wife with a skimpy food budget, a single mom with a skimpier food budget and three more mouths to feed and a volunteer at soup kitchens where people were grateful for something nourishing and hot. I picked up some mad skillz for combining food to make more out of less and make it out-fucking-standing. Hence what you have here in your hands.

This book is some grade-A, lazy person heaven. Just because you're too busy to make a five-course meal doesn't mean you should eat cat food every day of the week. I've compiled my best recipes that won't break the bank, take too long or taste like shit. Granny's got you covered.

Along the way, I also learned what I like and what I don't like. I don't eat what I don't like—not any more. Life's too fucking short for that. That said, as you read these recipes and plan your meals, leave out shit you don't like and add in shit you do like. Perfect shit every time!

Yes, I speak PottyMouth! My videos on YouTube and Facebook are super popular for it. You got a problem with that? Buy a different cookbook, dearie.

FAST AS FUCK RULES FOR LIFE

It doesn't take a fucking genius to put a delicious meal on the table in record time, but it does take some ingenuity, some prep and some planning. Don't freak out. I don't mean spreadsheets and shit, just a stocked pantry, a good idea of what you and your family will eat and the willingness to cut corners and give up the "from scratch" SuperCook cape.

FOUR PRINCIPLES WILL GUARANTEE FAST AS FUCK FOOD MAGIC IN YOUR LIFE.

(1) STOCK AND THEN REPLENISH YOUR PANTRY.

Store-bought, prepackaged, ready-mix or frozen are not cuss words. I'll throw plenty of real cuss words at you in here. No reason you can't be on good terms with food somebody else has already worked hard to make almost ready. When you find recipes that float your boat, write down the buy-ahead ingredients and put 'em on your shopping list. Each week buy what you can afford and then plan out your menus. A few days' worth of groceries in the cupboard will eliminate a frantic after-work run for takeout.

A stocked pantry is also your saving grace if you get sick, the weather turns ugly, unexpected guests show up in time to mooch a meal or any other disaster fucks up your plans. Soup is your best friend—trust me.

(2) DO SOME PREP AHEAD OF TIME.
Veggies already cut up or rice already cooked will save your ass on more than one occasion.

If you know you're gonna be short on time tomorrow, do some of the work today. Chopping or pre-mixing ingredients the night before will make your final assembly a fucking snap! Hungry doesn't wait for you to go all Grand Gourmet—just throw shit together, serve it warm or cold depending on the season, accept the compliments and then clean up later. FAST as FUCK is gonna be your middle name, and you're gonna love it.

(3) SPRINKLE IN FRESH SHIT AS TIME AND MONEY ALLOW.
Once a week or more, depending on how close you live to a grocery store, buy fresh fruits or veggies or bakery items to supplement the shit on your shelves. OR, if you have limited access to fresh ingredients, use them when you buy them and make enough for leftovers or freezer meals.

(4) EXPERIMENT FREELY.
Really? You need an explanation of this? Mix shit together that you really like and see what happens.

Peggy
AKA Granny

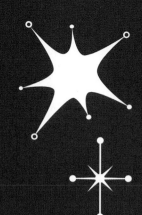

BREAKFAST BONANZA

I've never been one of those "I'll skip breakfast" kinda people. I need fuel to kick my ass into gear. I don't do coffee, I do FOOD! Breakfast for a bunch? Or a bunch of breakfasts? Take your pick. Yes, you've figured it out by now. I'd rather cook once and eat something for days in a row than have to cook every fucking day. OR, feed company with the same recipe. Double duty. You good with that?

For me, breakfast has always been a balance of protein and grains—but no cereal, please. Soggy shit in a bowl is NOT my idea of heaven. And forget sweets, no French toast or pancakes—sugar sets my gut into overdrive. No. Thank. You. Give me a casserole or a scramble or a sandwich, and I'm happy. So, here are some of my favorite make-ahead or make-in-a-hurry breakfast bonanzas. And, yes, for all you sugar freaks, I included a French toast abomination and a muffin-gasm recipe to die for. Eat up, you sweet fuckers.

OMELETTE MUFFINS

This is perfect for brunch when friends or family are visiting. For all the picky eaters in your bunch, you can make personalized Omelette Muffins—and relax over a cup of coffee or mimosas while they bake up in the oven. OR, if you're not a freakin' short-order cook, put in the shit you want, set them to bake and put your feet up and relax before your guests arrive. It's like a personalized omelette station, but with barely any work if you prep your filling the night before. And, they're so fuckin' cute, right?

MAKES 12

INGREDIENTS

6 large eggs

¾ cup (175 ml) milk—any kind will do

MY 5 FAVORITE FILLINGS (¼ CUP [60 G] EACH)

Precooked sausage links, diced

Tiny ham cubes

Zucchini and yellow crookneck squash, cubed

Leftover sautéed mushrooms

↳ **OR WHEN DESPERATE, I'LL OPEN A CAN OF SLICED ONES**

Shredded Colby/Jack cheese mix

MY VEGGIE FRIEND'S 5 FAVORITE FILLINGS (¼ CUP [60 G] EACH)

Leftover spinach, chopped small

↳ **OR FROZEN CHOPPED SPINACH**

Zucchini squash, chopped small

Orange bell pepper, chopped small

Yellow bell pepper, chopped small

Feta cheese

ASSEMBLY AND PREP

Preheat your oven to 350°F (177°C). If you don't trust your oven, invest in a reliable oven thermometer that you can take with you when you leave. Trust me: for this one, use paper muffin cups. Whisk the eggs and milk until frothy.

In a mixing bowl, combine all the desired fillings (except the cheese). Gently place a spoonful into each muffin cup, filling about three quarters full. Pour the beaten egg/milk into each muffin cup, leaving about ¼ inch (0.5 cm) for cheese. Don't stir. It'll all settle out, I promise. Sprinkle the cheese loosely on top of each mini casserole.

Bake for about 25 minutes until lightly browned on top. If it jiggles when you wiggle the pan, it's not done yet.

SERVE IT UP

Let the muffins sit in the pan for about 4 to 5 minutes so you can handle them. Serve alongside toast with homemade jam.

BONUS: These even taste okay at room temperature if you want to take them for lunch or to a function.

BONUS (AGAIN): Egg whites will work as well, but may require a bit more cooking time to set.

COCOA PUMPKIN MUFFIN-GASM

Yes, I have a thing for pumpkin. It's so fuckin' versatile for making shit moist and adding an unexpected flavor.

INGREDIENTS

1¾ cups (220 g) all-purpose flour

¼ tsp salt

1 tsp cocoa powder

1 tsp baking soda

1 tsp cinnamon

1 tsp nutmeg

⅔ cup (150 g) butter, softened

¾ cup (165 g) dark brown sugar, packed

⅓ cup (80 ml) molasses

1 egg, beaten, room temperature

1 cup (180 g) pumpkin purée

½ cup (40 g) smashed walnuts, optional

TO CRUNCH IT UP

Cream cheese or whipped cream, optional

PREP AND ASSEMBLY

Preheat the oven to 400°F (204°C) and grease a muffin tin or use cupcake papers.

In bowl #1, mix the flour, salt, cocoa, baking soda, cinnamon and nutmeg.

In bigger bowl #2, mix the butter, sugar and molasses with an electric mixer until light and fluffy. Add the egg and pumpkin, and blend well—but not until frothy.

Add about ½ cup (40 g) of the walnuts to the creamy mix and stir with a spatula. Gently fold the dry stuff from bowl #1 into the creamy pumpkin mixture. Use a spatula or a big spoon—DO NOT OVERMIX. Spoon into muffin tins.

Bake for 12 to 15 minutes and do the toothpick test—don't make me tell you again how to do it.

SERVE IT UP FANCY

If you wanna impress the fuck out of guests or have a muffin-gasm of your very own, serve them with cream cheese or whipped cream (or the pumpkin dip from page 65).

EGGS IN HASH POCKETS

Opening a can of corned beef hash to make a quick breakfast is NOT A CRIME! It's a coping strategy. So, let's make it fancy, okay? Remember the time when you ordered hash and eggs in a restaurant and they served it up all cutesy pie with the egg yolk staring at you from the center of the plate of hash? This is the version you can make at home.

SERVES 2-4

INGREDIENTS

1 (15-oz [425-g]) can corned beef hash, like Libby's

4 eggs

ASSEMBLE AND COOK

Using a large nonstick frying pan, spread the hash out in a thin layer all the way to the edges of the pan. Turn the heat to medium-low and start to warm the hash. With the back of a large cooking spoon, make 4 little indentations in the layer of mush. Gently drop one egg into each indentation. Break the yolks (or not) according to your preference. Keep the heat at medium-low, put a lid on the pan and let it top-stove bake for 4 to 6 minutes, depending on how well done you want your eggs to be.

SERVE IT UP

Use a VERY WIDE spatula to take out 4 individual portions of hash and egg. Done!

SOCAL HAM AND EGG SAMMIE

MAKES 1

McDonald's might have invented the Egg McMuffin, but people have been making ham and egg sandwiches for decades. The SoCal twist is to add smashed ripe avocado and use only egg whites. Oh, yeah. It's Yumville. Low cholesterol, high satisfaction.

INGREDIENTS

2–3 eggs, depending on your appetite

2 slices fresh sourdough bread, big slices

1 tbsp (15 g) mayonnaise

½ ripe avocado, sliced and mashed

2–3 slices of low-sodium ham

ASSEMBLE AND COOK

Separate the eggs and use only the whites. Fry them flat in a frying pan on medium-low heat and flip over like a crepe when just about done, about 2 to 3 minutes.

Toast the bread lightly and spread a thin layer of mayo on it. On one or both sides of the bread, spread a layer of mashed avocado. Spread the ham out evenly on the bread. Fold the fried egg white in half and lay on top of the ham. Finish it with the top slice of bread.

SERVE IT UP

Cut the sammie in half so it's easy to handle, and serve with a piece of fresh fruit. Enjoy your cup of joe, and then get on with your day.

PIZZA AND EGGS FOR BREAKFAST

OMFG—nothing makes me skip off to work feeling virtuous more than using up leftovers by throwing them in the frying pan in the morning for a quick egg-white scramble. Even a teaspoon of this and a smidgen of that will transform boring egg whites into something delightful. Remember the egg yolk scare of the 1970s? Cholesterol and all that shit? I quit eating egg yolks and haven't looked back (unless they're in a casserole and I can't tell the difference). I also hear that egg whites are the rage of all the fitness cookbooks, and I wanted to have something for everyone here.

SERVES 1

I have been known to put scrambled eggs on warmed-up leftover pizza slices and call it breakfast. Don't knock it if you haven't tried it. This also works as an evening meal. Nobody's gonna rat on you.

INGREDIENTS

2 slices of leftover Hawaiian pizza with Canadian bacon and lots of pineapple

OR OTHER PIZZA OF YOUR CHOICE

3 eggs

¼ cup (60 ml) milk

Pinch of salt and pepper

ASSEMBLE AND COOK

Heat the pizza in the toaster oven for about 2 minutes at 300°F (150°C). Lay them point end to crust end side-by-side on a plate, making a square.

Whisk together the eggs and milk, then scramble the eggs in a buttered frying pan over medium heat until no longer runny. Add some salt and pepper for good measure.

SERVE IT UP

Spread the scrambled eggs on top of the pizza so all traces of the pizza are covered.

You have my permission to grab a knife and fork and dig in. Wash it down with coffee, milk, a soda or a giant glass of juice. I really don't give a crap. Now, go about your day. Granny loves you.

SKINNY SCRAMBLE

I will forever defend my right to call shit breakfast if it includes scrambled or fried eggs. Leftovers, check. Fresh veggies, check. Chili and cheese, check. French fries and yesterday's burger—uh, not the burger, thanks. (Um, not tuna casserole, either, and not cold pizza.) But I am cool with all the ingredients you'd put on a pizza being in my breakfast eggs, so feel free to try it here. I know, I'm weird. Deal.

SERVES I, SOLO, UNO

INGREDIENTS

A few dabs of butter, divided

5–6 tbsp (approximately 50–60 g) of leftovers—whatever the fuck is in your fridge

SERIOUSLY. LEFTOVER ROAST BEEF? PEPPERONI? BROCCOLI? HOLY YUMNESS, THAT RIGHT THERE IS A GOOD START. WHAT'S HANGING OUT IN YOUR FRIDGE? PLEASE TELL ME YOU DID NOT THROW OUT THE LAST 4 BITES OF SAUTÉED SPINACH! THAT SHIT WOULD BE MAGICAL HERE WITH A CUT-UP TOMATO AND A SPRINKLE OF PARMESAN CHEESE.

3 large eggs, separated, whites only

Pinch of salt

Dash of pepper

ASSEMBLE AND COOK

Throw a dab of butter in a small frying pan and let it melt over medium heat. Warm up the leftovers in the melting butter for maybe 4 to 5 minutes max. Throw in another dab of butter until it melts. Keep the heat at medium. Gently pour the egg whites into the pan and either "omelette" it or stir it around with a plastic cooking fork if you want a true scramble. What's "omelette it"? Just pour it and let it sit, cover it for a few and then turn it over with a spatula. When the egg whites are no longer jiggling and are set to the consistency you like, you're done. On medium heat, this should be no more than 4 to 5 minutes. Add some salt and pepper if you want.

SERVE IT UP

Pour it into a bowl and chow down—with toast if you're not on a diet. Doctor it up with ketchup or hot sauce or whatever you like. Wash out the bowl and wipe out the frying pan—DONE, on your way. You're welcome.

TIP: It's cheaper to throw away the egg yolks than to buy egg whites from the store. Don't worry. We won't tell the chickens.

FRENCH TOAST CASSEROLE

Okay, this is for all you whiny butts who want to start your day with a sugar shot. Don't blame me if you end up in a fuckin' food coma an hour after you finish eating.

BASE
1 loaf of French bread

➤ *DEFINITELY TRY THIS WITH CHALLAH OR HAWAIIAN BREAD*

Butter (for the baking dish)

8 eggs, beaten

1 pt (475 ml) half and half

1 cup (235 ml) milk

3 tbsp (35 g) sugar

1½ tsp (7 ml) vanilla extract

½ tsp ground cinnamon

⅛ tsp ground nutmeg

Pinch of salt—that literally means pinch a tiny bit between your thumb and first finger

CINNAMON CRUNCH TOPPING
12 tbsp butter (1½ sticks [170 g]), softened, so you can mix shit into it

➤ *DON'T GO CHEAP ON THIS. NO WHIPPED BUTTER, NO MARGARINE. REAL BUTTER.*

1 cup (220 g) brown sugar, jam-packed into a measuring cup

1 tbsp (15 ml) light corn syrup

➤ *HONEY OR PANCAKE SYRUP WILL WORK JUST AS WELL*

1 tsp ground cinnamon

½ tsp ground nutmeg

OPTIONAL
Fruit, chocolate chips, sprinkles, etc.

PREP AND ASSEMBLY (THE NIGHT BEFORE)
Slice the bread diagonally into pieces about 1 inch (2.5 cm) thick. Generously butter a 9 x 13–inch (23 x 33–cm) baking dish. In a large bowl, whisk together the eggs, half and half, milk, sugar, vanilla extract, cinnamon, nutmeg and salt until well blended, but don't overbeat. Dip each slice of bread into the egg mixture and arrange in the pan in two rows. The first piece should be standing but leaning back against the side of the baking dish. Continue dipping and layering the slices until you have two rows of approximately 10 slices each. Pour the remaining egg mixture evenly over the dipped slices of bread. Cover the baking dish with aluminum foil and refrigerate overnight.

For the topping, combine all the ingredients together in a medium-sized bowl until well blended. Cover and refrigerate overnight.

COOK THAT SHIT UP (IN THE MORNING)
Preheat the oven to 350°F (177°C). Spread the cinnamon crunch topping evenly over the top of the casserole and bake for about 35 minutes or until the casserole is puffed and light golden brown. Watch it like a hawk. That sugar will burn if you cook it too hot or too long.

SERVE IT—AND STRETCH IT
Lay out some toppings, dessert-bar style: bananas, strawberries, blueberries, chocolate chips, sprinkles, etc. If people want a sugar high, you might as well go all the way.

MEAT? YOU WANT MEAT?

If you love meat, these'll make you happy. Back in my childhood days, we had neighborhood butcher shops where you always knew the meat had been humanely grown and was clean and antibiotic free. Many large grocery chains now offer meat that echoes those 1950s standards. You'll pay a tiny bit more—and for me, it's worth it. I personally buy meat without GMOs, hormones or high fat content. For lots of reasons (climate sensitivity, budget, body weight, heart health and the fact that I thrive on variety), I like to mix it up—chicken, fish, beef, pork and LOTS of veggies. But, hey, this is a recipe book, not a manifesto or your marching orders. Fix shit you like, and it will be just fine.

'TWAS THE NIGHT BEFORE . . . CHILI

Three pounds (1.4 kg) of meat, some seasonings, a little prep time, a bit of warming time and you can sit down to a bowl of chili that'll wiggle your fuckin' socks. This is a do-ahead meal AND a leftovers-for-days meal—a twofer! Personalize this any way you wish. Carb it up or leave it plain; either way it's tummy-pleasing and easy as fuck.

MAIN INGREDIENTS

2 lbs (0.9 kg) chili meat

TIP: ASK THE BUTCHER FOR CHILI GRIND—IT'S LUMPIER THAN REGULAR MINCE.

1 lb (455 g) ground pork

ANY DEPTH GRIND WILL DO

1 tbsp (15 g) onion salt

1 tsp garlic powder, if you like it

2 (16-oz [455-g]) cans no- or low-salt beef broth, divided

3 (8-oz [225-g]) cans tomato sauce, such as Hunt's

SPICE IT UP

2 tsp (10 g) salt

3 tsp (7 g) paprika

2¼ tsp (5 g) cumin

1 tsp oregano

6 tbsp (45 g) chili powder

1 tbsp (12 g) sugar

OPTIONAL ADD-INS

1 (16-oz [455-g]) can pinto beans

1 (16-oz [455-g]) can puréed tomatoes, no discernible skins

¼ tsp allspice

Hot peppers

Additional meat

PORK, BEEF, CHICKEN—IN PULLED FORM TO ADD TO THE TEXTURE

OPTIONAL TOPPINGS

Grated Jack cheese

Raw onions

Salsa

Sour cream

Jalapeño peppers

Corn chips

PREP AND ASSEMBLY

Sear the beef and pork chili meats with the onion salt and garlic powder until no liquid remains in the frying pan. (Note: you might have to do it in 2 batches if your pan is too friggin' small.) Stir constantly to make sure it breaks up and cooks thoroughly.

Mix the rest of the dry spices together in a measuring cup or bowl to blend them well. Sprinkle the spices on the cooked meat, mixing well. Stir around in the frying pan for 10 more minutes and dump that shit in a big-ass bowl. Add one can of beef broth and the tomatoes; stir. Depending on your personal preference for chili (thick or runny), you may need to add the second can of broth. Cover and place in the fridge overnight. This mingles the flavors and creates the magic.

COOK

Slow cooker method: Add in any extras and set it on low just before you leave for the day. House is gonna smell like a chili-gasm when you get home (as long as it's only 8 to 10 hours). Top with whatever and dig in.

Stovetop method: Add in any extras and warm it up on low heat for about 30 minutes while you change out of your work clothes. You even have time to start a load of laundry or do some other bullshit chore. Then top with some extra crap and dig in.

MEATY SPAGHETTI SAUCE

OMFG—A real Italian dude gave my spaghetti sauce his blessing. He should. I made a small tweak to improve the recipe he gave me. Yes, it's that fucking good, and you can use it sooooo many ways. Add meat to it, add meatballs to it and freeze it in one-cup (235-ml) pouches for adding to soup, other recipes or for a homemade pizza night. You can even freeze it in an ice-cube tray for adding to breakfast eggs.

SERVES 10-12

INGREDIENTS

1 tbsp (15 g) bacon fat or about 4 strips of bacon

1 (6-oz [170-g]) can tomato paste

5–10 sprigs Italian parsley, chopped

NOT CILANTRO, NOT REGULAR PARSLEY

2 (28-oz [795-g]) cans crushed tomatoes

2 (28-oz [795-g]) cans tomato sauce

1 tbsp (2 g) Italian seasoning

¼ tsp each salt and pepper

2 tbsp (24 g) sugar

I TBSP (12 G) AT A TIME, TEST IT

½ cup (90 g) grated Parmesan cheese

1 lb (455 g) flank steak or stew beef

OPTIONAL

Meatballs (page 30) or Italian sausage

ASSEMBLY AND PREP

In a big-ass pot, heat the bacon grease or cook the bacon. Leave the grease and remove the bacon. Sauté the tomato paste and chopped parsley in the heated bacon grease. When properly sautéed (a few minutes), add the crushed tomatoes and tomato sauce. Stir to get a consistent texture. Now add the Italian seasoning, salt, pepper and half the sugar; stir and taste. Add more sugar if needed. Let it simmer for about 30 minutes. Then add the grated Parmesan cheese to taste. Stir and simmer another 10 minutes.

ADDING MEAT OR MEATBALLS

Slice the flank steak into walnut-sized pieces or use stewing beef. Brown it evenly and then plop it into the pan so that it cooks in the simmering sauce. You want the meat to cook as long as possible to add flavor and become tender, even shredding over time.

If you plan to add meatballs and/or sausage to the sauce, do it about 30 minutes before you serve the sauce—longer than that and they become tough.

SERVE IT UP

Big bowls, forks and twirling spoons. *Mangia mangia.*

MEATBALLS

There's nothing more versatile than a meatball or meatloaf recipe—and each family has their own—but I happen to think mine is the best fuckin' one on the planet, cuz even the Italians in my circle of friends have begged for the recipe. I can't hide it any longer. Here it is—easy as fuck, fast as fuck, simple as fuck. And listen, don't bitch about making three pounds (1.4 kg) of these little fuckers. Freeze what you don't eat right away. One night when you're starving, you'll be so glad you did. Meatball sandwich with some of the leftover spaghetti sauce? Pizza topping? Whatever!

MAKES 5 DOZEN MINIS, 3 DOZEN MEDIUM

INGREDIENTS

1 cello pack of saltine crackers

OR

1 cup (160 g) cooked brown rice, for gluten free

3 large eggs

¾ cup (175 ml) ketchup

1 tsp brown mustard

OR YELLOW IF YOU MUST

1 tbsp (15 ml) Worcestershire sauce

3 tbsp (45 ml) steak sauce, such as A-1

2 lbs (0.9 kg) really good ground beef, 10% fat if you can find it

1 lb (455 g) ground turkey, low fat content

ASSEMBLY AND PREP

Put the whole cello pack of saltines into a large plastic bag and smash it into tiny crumbs. In a medium bowl, crack the eggs and add the liquid ingredients. Whisk well. Now add the crumbs (or the rice) to the liquid mush and let it sit for a tiny bit.

Meanwhile, in another bowl, mix the two kinds of meat well—kneading and squishing through your fingers. Now, mix in the crumbs/liquid paste and work it thoroughly into the meat mixture.

BAKE

Preheat the oven to 325°F (163°C).

Make little balls for cocktail meatballs or medium balls for spaghetti meatballs. Really? You need to know how to make a ball? Pinch off about a teaspoon's worth, and roll it around in your palms. Voila!

Spread them out on a cookie sheet and bake for about 20 minutes (little) or 25 minutes (medium). Because you used really good meat, these won't leak grease.

DONE

Now, put 'em in spaghetti sauce, in sweet/sour sauce for a party appetizer or freeze 'em for whatever pleases your little pea brain when you're hungry.

BAD-ASS BEEF AND BROCCOLI

Plain old beef and broccoli just doesn't cut it for me. I need more veggies, more texture and more color. I hope you can buy sugar snap peas where you live (the kind you see in your food when you go to a Chinese restaurant). Who needs fancy schmancy spices when everything you need is inside a bottle of Asian salad dressing? Oh, yum.

SERVES 4-6

INGREDIENTS

A splash of olive oil for the wok

1 lb (455 g) sirloin steak, sliced thin

1 (10-oz [285-g]) bag frozen broccoli

¼ cup (40 g) fresh sugar snap peas, cut up

1 carrot, sliced ultra thin

1 orange, red or yellow bell pepper, sliced ultra thin

¾ cup (175 ml) Asian sesame salad dressing

Cooked white or brown rice for serving

Soy sauce, optional

ASSEMBLE AND COOK

Use a wok that's big enough so that all the food can move easily. Heat the pan to medium-high, then throw in the oil and the steak bits. Cook the meat for just a minute. Add the veggies and the salad dressing; stir thoroughly. Turn the heat down to medium and keep stirring until the broccoli is tender, 4 to 6 minutes.

SERVE IT UP

Pour that shit right outta the wok onto a pile of white or brown rice. See how pretty it is with a little bit of color from the carrots and the pepper? Add soy sauce if you must, but at least taste it first. I told you, right? BAD ASS to the max!

EFFIN AMAZING CHICKEN

SERVES 4-6

This takes a maximum 10 minutes of prep and then a little over an hour of cooking while you settle in from a day at work. Do chores, exercise or homework—or take a few minutes for yourself—while this cooks. So simple, so full of flavor—fuck, yeah!

INGREDIENTS

1 (10-oz [285-g]) can cream of mushroom soup (low salt)

1 (10-oz [285-g]) can cream of chicken soup (low salt)

➤ *LOTS OF SALT IN THE DRY MIXES, HENCE THE LOW-SALT SOUP*

1 soup can of water for moist rice

1 cup-ish (75 g) of mushrooms, fresh or canned, chopped

1 (1- to 2-oz [30- to 55-g]) packet of either onion soup mix or ranch-style dressing mix

2 cups (320 g) cooked rice

➤ *WHITE, BROWN OR INTEGRATED*

1 lb (455 g) boneless, skinless chicken

➤ *THIGHS ARE JUICIER*

Salt and pepper

Sprigs of rosemary, for garnish

ASSEMBLY AND PREP

Grease up a 9 x 13–inch (23 x 33–cm) baking pan. Preheat the oven to 325°F (163°C).

In a big-ass bowl, mix the 2 cans of soup and one can of water. Whisk until blended. Add the mushrooms and your choice of onion soup mix or dry ranch-style dressing mix. Whisk again. Mix the cooked rice into what's working in your big-ass bowl by now. Stir with a sturdy spoon or spatula. Pour the mixture into the buttered pan. Arrange the raw chicken on top of the rice mixture. Sprinkle with salt and pepper. Cover the pan with foil and bake for 60 to 70 minutes.

RELAX

You can probably get two loads of laundry and half of the homework done while this bakes up. OR, have a glass of wine and tuck into your favorite magazine, book or Granny video.

SERVE IT UP

Serve right out of the pan using a wide spatula. Toss a sprig of rosemary on top. Pick your family's favorite vegetable or serve with a salad for a fucking FDA-approved balanced meal.

TIP: I have tried this with onion soup mix (zingy), and I have tried it with ranch-style dressing mix. My favorite is a combo of half a packet each. Zowie, it just sets my taste buds into overdrive.

CRISPY PESTO CHICKEN

I had pesto chicken pizza one day and was surprised by how much I liked it. The flavors work together. So I dreamed up this main-dish adaptation with a panko crunch and the understated taste of pesto—chicken all dressed up for a date, if you will. So, be on your best behavior. Manners and shit. As always, it's the combo of unexpected flavor and multiple textures that really gets my taste buds all aflutter. You'll love this.

SERVES 4

INGREDIENTS

½ cup (120 g) prepared pesto sauce

➤ *OR STORE-BOUGHT IF YOU DON'T MAKE YOUR OWN*

1 cup (120 g) panko bread crumbs

4 chicken leg/thigh combos or breasts, skin off

½ cup (60 g) shredded mozzarella cheese for last 5 minutes of baking

ASSEMBLY AND PREP

Preheat the oven to 350°F (177°C) and grease up a cookie sheet. Lay out a shallow bowl and fill it with the pesto sauce. Lay out another shallow bowl or dish, or use a plastic bag for the panko crumbs. Pat the chicken pieces dry with a paper towel. Then dunk each piece into the pesto sauce 'til it's covered. Now dip right into the panko crumbs and gently place on the cookie sheet. Bake uncovered about 25 to 30 minutes (big pieces take longer). When you think it's done, sprinkle the mozzarella cheese on top. Now, give it 5 more minutes in the oven for some melty amazingness.

SERVE IT UP

Pull it outta the oven and put it right on your plates. Serve with pasta or rice and a veggie side—whatever you want.

NOTE: The panko crumbs don't stay crispy for leftovers—jus' sayin'.

GRANNY'S FAMOUS CHICKEN CACCIATORE

SERVES 4

You already know I'm a freak for Italian food (oh, and Mexican, too). This no-fail chicken cacciatore is a HUGE crowd pleaser and a super easy first-date meal. You don't need to worry too much about timing and it's bound to impress. All you need to worry about is your manners while slurping pasta. Try egg noodles instead of spaghetti. Much easier to manage gracefully.

● ●

INGREDIENTS

½ cup (120 ml) Italian salad dressing

3 lbs (1.4 kg) chicken legs and thighs, skin off

1 tsp garlic powder, if you like it

¼ tsp Italian seasoning

1–2 loose carrots, sliced

1 yellow onion, chopped

1 each of red and green pepper, chopped

1½ cups (100 g) sliced fresh mushrooms

1 (28-oz [795-g]) can diced or crushed tomatoes

Egg noodles, for the full effect

ASSEMBLE AND COOK

Grab a big-ass deep skillet or wok, and pour the Italian salad dressing into it. Turn the heat to medium and cook the chicken pieces until browned evenly, 2 to 3 minutes per side. Sprinkle the garlic powder and Italian seasoning evenly. Add the carrots, onion, peppers and mushrooms. Stir for 4 to 5 minutes. Pour the tomatoes over the whole mess and then slap a cover on that pan. Turn the heat to low and let it simmer for about 30 to 35 more minutes. Cook some pasta on another stove burner, and you'll be ready for *mangia mangia*.

SERVE IT UP

Ladle that dreamy chicken concoction over the pasta and prepare to be transported to Italy.

HANGOVER CHICKEN

So, the real reason I named this hangover chicken is because—well—beer, tomato juice and pimento-stuffed olives. You wouldn't think this shit would go well together, but it's frickin' amazing. This is a slow-cooking meal. I've never made it on top of the stove, so if you do, you're on your own.

INGREDIENTS

1 (12-oz [355-ml]) can beer, any shit will do

1 (16-oz [475-ml]) can tomato juice

NOT V8

1½ cups (100 g) sliced fresh mushrooms

3 lbs (1.4 kg) chicken legs and thighs, skin off

1 (8-oz [225-g]) jar pimento-stuffed green olives

ASSEMBLY AND PREP

Dump the beer and tomato juice into a slow cooker. Add the mushrooms. Add the chicken pieces. Add the whole jar of olives, juice and all. Put the lid on, turn it to low. It'll be ready in 8 to 9 hours. You'll be able to tell it's ready when you see the meat fall off the bones. DON'T open the lid to sniff. You'll break the steaming Karma.

SERVE IT UP

Ladle that amazingness over some pasta or rice, and there ya go.

NO PEEK CHICKEN (OR PORK)

Okay, okay, I know this one looks similar, but the taste is completely different. Trust me, okay?

Max 15 minutes of prep, then 2 plus hours of cooking while you go about your day. If you've had your fill of chicken, fine—use thinly sliced pork steaks with all the fat trimmed off. Either way, it's a big fuck yeah!

SERVES 4-6

INGREDIENTS

1 (6-oz [170 g]) box Uncle Ben's Long Grain Wild Rice (original recipe)

1 (10.5-oz [298-g]) can cream of mushroom soup (low salt)

1 (10.5-oz [298-g]) can cream of celery soup (low salt)

2 soup cans of water

About 1 lb (455 g) chicken breasts, tenders or boneless thighs

1 large stalk of fresh broccoli (as big as a baby's head), chopped

ASSEMBLY AND PREP

Grease up a 9 x 13–inch (23 x 33–cm) baking pan. Preheat the oven to 325°F (163°C).

In a medium bowl, mix the box of rice, cans of soup and two cans of water. Pour the mixture into the buttered pan. Arrange the raw chicken on top of the rice mixture. Arrange the broccoli florets around the edges of the pan. Cover the pan with foil and bake for 2½ hours.
DO NOT peek at it or lift the foil.

RELAX

This is another one of those day-off recipes, so hang out doing what you do while this fills the entire house with delicious aromas.

SERVE IT UP

Serve right out of the pan using a wide spatula. Some fresh rolls and a salad, and you've got a fuckin' banquet, restaurant style.

OVEN CHICKEN NACHOS

Homemade nachos—I'm in Mexi-Heaven. Super easy whether you cook the chicken yourself or snag a precooked one from the grocery store on the way home. It probably seems silly to have a recipe this simple in a cookbook, FCOL, but I've had more than one under-25 person marvel at the magic of my nachos when I put 'em on the table. "How'd you do that?" I just smile sweetly and tell 'em it's a closely guarded family secret. Shred, spread, heat and eat. Fuck yeah!

SERVES 6

● ●

INGREDIENTS

3–4 cups (270–360 g) of your favorite tortilla chips

1 or 2 (8-oz [130-g]) bags of Mexican blend cheese or 1 cup (130 g) each of Monterey Jack and Cheddar cheese

2 cups (460 g) chopped or shredded already-cooked chicken

TOPPINGS

Sour cream

Salsa

Jalapeños

Hot sauce

ASSEMBLY AND PREP

Preheat the oven to 350°F (177°C) and grease up a 9 x 13–inch (23 x 33–cm) glass casserole dish. Starting with the chips, layer that shit with love. Chips, cheese, chicken—see how it all has that *ch* goin' on? Put one final thin layer of cheese on top so you can watch it. Pop it in the oven for 10 to 12 minutes, or until the top layer of cheese is bubbly and melted.

SERVE IT UP

Let it cool for 5 minutes so you don't burn the fuck outta the roof of your mouth. Spoon it outta the casserole with a spatula, and dig in. Load your favorite yummy shit on top. Whoa. Tasty City. Fingers are awesome. Keep napkins handy.

SWEET POTATO AND CHICKEN GET MARRIED ON A RANCH (DRESSING, THAT IS)

SERVES 4

So, seriously, is there anything that doesn't go with chicken? I have a good buddy who's gaga for sweet potatoes, and when trying to dream up something that she'd like, I remembered that she was also nutso for ranch dressing. She likes onions, but I can't fault her for that—we all have our thing, ya know. I told her it was an experiment when she walked in the front door, but she said she was already won over by the aroma. Phew. It turned out great, and it's fast, easy and fucking delicious.

INGREDIENTS

4 chicken leg/thigh combos or full breasts, skin off

2 sweet potatoes, peeled and cubed to about walnut size

1 sweet onion, cut into wedges

½ (0.5 oz [14 g]) packet of ranch dressing seasoning

½ tbsp (7 ml) olive oil or cooking spray

ASSEMBLY AND PREP

Preheat the oven to 350°F (177°C) and grease up a cookie sheet. Put all the ingredients into a big zip-top bag and shake it like you mean it. Make sure the ranch dressing seasoning is all over everything. Spread that shit on the cookie sheet. It's okay if they touch. They're married. Bake uncovered about 30 to 35 minutes. You'll know it's done when the sweet potatoes are tender.

SERVE IT UP

Pull it outta the oven and put it right on your plates. Serve with pasta or rice and a side salad—whatever you want.

NOTE: This is a bomb take-to-work leftover.

GREATEST PORK CHOPS EVER

Lots of people make BBQ'd pork ribs, right? And a bunch more people eat applesauce alongside pork roast, right? Well, I decided to combine the best of both of those scenarios, and my friends call these the GREATEST—well, they really say they're the FUCKING GREATEST, but I didn't want to brag too much.

● ●

INGREDIENTS

A splash of olive oil for the frying pan

4 boneless pork chops, cheapest cut

½ cup (120 ml) of your favorite BBQ sauce

2 or 3 sweet apples, cored, peeled, chopped

White or brown rice for serving, optional

ASSEMBLE AND COOK

Pick out a skillet that's big enough so that all the pork will fit in one layer. Make sure the pan has a lid. Heat the pan to medium; then throw in the oil and the pork chops. Cook the pork chops to a nice golden brown on both sides, about 3 minutes per side. Add the BBQ sauce and the chopped apple bits. Turn the heat down to medium-low, cover the pan and simmer for 20 minutes.

SERVE IT UP

Pour that shit right outta the pan onto a pile of white or brown rice. Side of your favorite vegetable, and you're experiencing the greatest pork chops EVER.

You're welcome very much.

GRANNY'S SIGNATURE SHIT

If you hang around with the same pals for a while, you go to a shit-ton of potluck gatherings. And, if you have nice friends, they let you know which shit you brought that was awesome (and the really good friends will tell you which shit sucked).

Over the years, I've become known for these things—everything from my number one requested sweet-and-sour meatballs to my squash pickles. If you wanna be top o' the heap at the potlucks in your crowd, try some of these (unless they're already somebody else's signature dishes).

Should we have a taste-off of potluck contributions? Hmmmm.

GRANNY'S FAMOUS SWEET & SOUR SAUCE

Back in nineteen and fifty-something, kids, I was a Girl Scout. And one of our badges was cooking. And for that badge, we fixed a recipe that made our 1950s families swoon. Sweet and sour sauce with two ingredients: cranberry sauce and grape jelly. Oh, and we added teenie weenies to it. GAG a maggot! I ate that shit for decades until I realized I could spice it up a bit and make it my own. I'm firmly convinced you'll like this version better. All my friends do. And, yes, pineapple. Deal!

MAKES 1 QUART (1 L)

SAUCE INGREDIENTS

2 (12-oz [340-g]) bottles chili sauce

NOT COCKTAIL SAUCE, NOT KETCHUP

1 (14-oz [395-g]) can whole-berry cranberry sauce

1 (20-oz [565-g]) can crushed pineapple, with liquid

½ cup (175 g) pancake syrup

SHIT YOU DUMP INTO THE SAUCE

Meatballs (page 30)

Chicken drumettes

BAKE COVERED AT 325°F [163°C] FOR 30 MINUTES BEFORE PUTTING THEM IN THE SAUCE

Teenie weenies (mini hot dogs) right outta the can

ASSEMBLY AND PREP

I'm dying here at having to write up directions for this shit. The portions in the ingredients list are for a double batch—enough for the 5 dozen meatballs from page 30.

Seriously, open the cans and bottles, warm up the shit until the cranberry sauce is no longer in the shape of a can, stir it all together and then plop in the meatballs or chicken drumettes or teenie weenies or whatever-the-fuck you want. Let the shit sit in the goop for at least an hour on super low heat (slow cooker or top of stove), and you're the hero of the potluck. See extra instructions in the ingredients list if you're using chicken drumettes.

Trust me, it's that easy. Just don't overdo it with the heat or you'll burn it. Sugar, ya know?

HAWAIIAN FRUIT SALAD

I like everything about this except the coconut. I know, I know. I've already admitted it. I'm defective. So, if you like it, add it. If you don't like it, leave it out. Your food, your choice. Mwah. I'm lucky to have visited Hawaii several times in my lifetime. The fruit there is kissed by the sun, the moisture and the warm climate. Oh my goodness. Fortunately for those who don't live there, you can often find these delicious fruits in frozen form in your local grocery store. Yummmmmm. Go for it. Peeps love it when I show up with this at a potluck.

SERVES 6-8

INGREDIENTS

1 fresh pineapple

OR BAG OF FROZEN CHUNKS

2 fresh kiwi, peeled and sliced

2 mangoes, peeled and chunked

2 bananas, medium ripe

1 guava, peeled and chunked

1 tangerine, peeled and sectioned

1 apple, peeled and thinly sliced

1 cup (150 g) strawberries, fresh or frozen (thawed), sliced

OR ANY OTHER FRUIT YOU LIKE IF YOU DON'T LIVE IN ALOHALAND.

Shredded coconut for serving

Macadamia nuts for serving, optional

ASSEMBLY AND PREP

Mix everything all up and sprinkle it with coconut (if you like that shit).

SERVE IT UP

Lay it out pretty on a platter or mix it all up in a bowl—your choice. Serve some macadamia nuts in a little side dish, put on some slack-key music and enjoy.

> **NOTE:** If you're old-school USA Midwest church supper, you probably think this thing calls for Cool Whip and marshmallows. NO, don't do that. Fruit is all you need. Do not mistake this for crappy "ambrosia" church-supper style.

GREEN BEAN SALAD

By itself, this is a great addition to a potluck. At home, with or without guests, this can turn any summer night into instant supper with the addition of a few other nibbles. I like to serve this garnished with hard-boiled eggs, a side of cubed ham and a few strawberries. Yes, I know, I'm a freak for mixing textures and tastes. Here you've got vinegar, sweet, salty—and then you've got smushy, soft, strawberry seeds. It fuckin' works, right? Add some cheese and crackers, and you've got the makings of a swanky picnic.

SERVES 10-12

INGREDIENTS

4 lbs (1.8 kg) fresh green beans, cut into 1-in (2.5-cm) lengths

1 lb (455 g) fresh yellow beans, cut into 1-in (2.5-cm) lengths

1 (8-oz [225-g]) package frozen baby lima beans

1 (10.5-oz [300-g]) can garbanzo beans

1 (10.5-oz [300-g]) can kidney beans

1 red bell pepper, chopped very fine

1 whole bunch (200 g) of celery, chopped medium

1 bunch (75 g) of green onions, chopped small, if you like that shit

DRESSING

1 cup (235 ml) rice vinegar

1 cup (235 ml) olive oil

1 tbsp (12 g) sugar

1 tbsp (8 g) black pepper

1 tbsp (15 g) salt

¼ tsp garlic powder, if you can't live without garlic

¼ tsp onion powder, if you don't use fresh onions

¼ tsp Italian seasoning

ASSEMBLY AND PREP

Blanch the fresh beans for 3 to 4 minutes, depending on how tender you like them. Drain them well and dry them on paper towels so the dressing will stick. Cook the frozen lima beans for 10 minutes; then drain, cool and dry.

Mix all the dressing ingredients in a bowl and whisk well so everything gets along together. Combine all the beans and chopped veggies with the dressing, and stir until everything is coated. Chill the salad at least 4 hours before serving.

SERVE IT UP

Put the bowl of bean salad on the table with a slotted spoon so peeps can serve themselves. Lay out other ingredients and let people pick what they want. If you're taking this to a potluck, drain most of the dressing and save for your own salad at home.

TIP: If you wanna go catering-style fancy with this, spoon it into a hollowed-out head of lettuce or hollowed-out bell peppers. Let your imagination go wild.

FUNERAL POTATOES (FOR THE LIVING)

Do yourself a favor and find Kate Campbell's song "Funeral Food," and you'll understand this recipe even better. Truly, make these for any occasion, not just a funeral reception. Oh, and while we're talking about potlucks, PLEASE take these already warmed up so that you don't stress out the host or hostess. Invest in one of those insulated casserole carriers, or wrap this in a beach towel and take it in a cardboard box.

SERVES 10-12

Oh, and if you just love the taste of this amazingness, fix it for dinner and serve it with anything else you like. Yummmmmmmy.

INGREDIENTS

1 (28- to 32-oz [795- to 905-g]) bag frozen, shredded hash brown potatoes

8 tbsp (1 stick [115 g]) salted butter

½ medium onion, finely diced

¼ cup (30 g) all-purpose flour

1 cup (235 ml) milk

2 cups (475 ml) low-sodium chicken broth

1 tsp each of salt and pepper

1½ cups (195 g) grated Monterey Jack cheese

1 cup (120 g) sour cream

½ cup (60 g) grated sharp cheddar

2 cups (70 g) crumbled potato chips, packed lightly

¼ cup (45 g) grated Parmesan cheese

ASSEMBLY AND PREP

Thaw the frozen potatoes in the fridge overnight or on the counter for a few hours. Preheat the oven to 325°F (163°C). Grease up a big 11 x 14–inch (28 x 35–cm) casserole dish or a disposable metal pan.

Mix EVERYTHING except the chips and Parmesan cheese in your favorite big-ass bowl. Dump the shit into the dish or metal pan. Mix the crumbled potato chips with the Parmesan cheese. Sprinkle that on top. Bake uncovered for 35 to 40 minutes. Done. Show up to the potluck and be a hero.

SERVE IT UP

If you're taking it to a potluck in the disposable pan, try to take a disposable spoon, too. Otherwise, don't send your best serving spoon, cuz it might get confused during cleanup.

People do know how to serve themselves out of a potluck pan. Trust me.

THREE-CORN CASSEROLE

I know, I know, this is a calorie and artery BOMB! Make it for a potluck so you get only a spoonful. No need to fuck yourself up with guilt by making this at home. Uh, did you hear me? I said POTLUCK! I think my version is slightly better than the Jiffy version, because, well, cream cheese. Ya know?

SERVES 12–14, POTLUCK STYLE

INGREDIENTS

2 large eggs

1 (8-oz [225-g]) box Jiffy cornbread mix

1 (15-oz [425-g]) can creamed corn

1 (15-oz [425-g]) can whole-kernel corn, drained

½ cup (115 g) butter, melted

½ cup (120 g) cream cheese

MELTED WITH THE BUTTER

½ cup (60 g) sour cream

Monterey Jack cheese, optional

Jalapeños, optional

ASSEMBLY AND PREP

Preheat the oven to 350°F (177°C) and grease up a 9 x 9–inch (23 x 23–cm) glass casserole dish. Mix everything together at once, except the Jack cheese and jalapeños, in a big-ass bowl. Put it all in the casserole dish. Could it be any easier?

Bake about an hour, uncovered, and do the toothpick test.

SERVE IT UP

Pull it outta the oven and take it to the effin' potluck. Ya know what? It also goes well with a Mexican-themed dinner. If you really wanna go nuts, sprinkle a little Jack cheese on each serving.

NOTE: If you wanna fuck with people who aren't expecting it, add a couple of small cans of jalapeño peppers to this shit. Chop 'em small so they can't escape them.

NO BURP BREAD & BUTTER PICKLES

I bet you think that canning, pickling and jamming are just for the Stepford wives, right? WRONG, my little fuckers. ANYBODY can do it. This is the easiest no-burp pickles recipe EVER. One day I was eating lunch in a very froufrou, ladies-who-eat-lunch sorta place—and I was served bliss-in-every-bite pickles alongside my sandwich. Even though they looked like cucumbers, they didn't taste like it, and I didn't get the burps. It took me a couple of tries to get this recipe right, but, oh, man. Yum City! Okay, so it's not FAST as FUCK, but it's easy and each step is painless, so I included it cuz my friends love these and I figured you would, too.

MAKES 4-6 JARS

SUPPLIES

1 medium pan for prepping the veggies

1 colander

6 pint-size (475-ml) canning jars with lids

1 set of canning tools

1 BIG-ASS pan with a wire rack in the bottom, if you choose to heat process

INGREDIENTS

⅓ cup (80 g) salt

6 medium zucchini or crookneck squash, sliced ¼ in (0.5 cm) thick

2 red onions, roughly chopped

IN MY PICKLES, I TAKE OUT THE ONIONS BEFORE PRESERVING, CUZ I DON'T LIKE 'EM, BUT I DO LIKE THE FLAVOR THEY IMPART DURING THE BRINING.

2 cups (385 g) sugar

3 cups (710 ml) cider vinegar

1 tsp celery seed

1 tsp turmeric

½ tsp mustard seed

EASY STEPS

#1 Make a brine by pouring the salt into 1 quart (945 ml) of water in the medium pan. Soak the sliced zucchini, or crookneck squash, and onions in the salted water. Add a little water to cover if necessary. Stir it around gently just once or twice. Let the veggies sit still in the brine for 3 hours.

#2 Drain and rinse the squash/onion mixture using the colander.

#3 Boil the sugar, vinegar, celery seed, turmeric and mustard seed in the medium pan for 5 minutes.

#4 Add the drained veggies and bring to a simmer for no more than 2 to 3 minutes.

#5 Ladle the veggie mixture into canning jars.

#6 Then either store the jars in the refrigerator or process in a water bath canner (the BIG-ASS pan).

RELAX

This is another one of those day-off recipes. The first part takes about 15 minutes of prep and 3 hours of waiting. Steps 2 to 5 take about 30 minutes. Step 6 takes either no time at all (refrigerator) or 30 minutes (water bath). If you've been dying to try preserving food, this is your easiest shot. Trust me, you'll be so proud of what you've accomplished.

THREE-INGREDIENT POTATO SALAD

SERVES 10-15

OMG, you've been invited to a giant potluck and your budget is stretched, your time is jammed, and yet you don't want to show up empty-handed like some mooching fucker! I've got your back, kids. This has surprisingly full-bodied flavor thanks to the ranch dressing, which effectively lets you get by without cutting up onions or adding garlic or parsley cuz they're all already in the dressing. Adding fresh celery amps up the texture meter and keeps you from looking lazy.

INGREDIENTS

2 (30-oz [850-g]) bags frozen cube-style hash brown potatoes

1 large stalk of fresh celery, chopped super tiny

1 (15-oz [445-ml]) jar ranch-style dressing, pick your favorite brand

Salt and pepper to taste

ASSEMBLY AND PREP

In a giant-ass pan, boil enough water that you can cover the potatoes. Dump 'em in the water and cook for no more than 10 minutes.

After 10 minutes in the boiling water, the potatoes are fine. Drain them. Put the potatoes in a HUGE-ass bowl and immediately slather with the dressing. Fold in the chopped celery, add salt and pepper to taste and you're done.

SERVE IT UP

The first time I made this, I put it in a large throwaway baking pan and decorated it as if it were a beach scene. I used the leafy tops of the celery stalks to simulate palm trees. I cut 4 or 5 cherry tomatoes in half and spread them around to look like beach umbrellas, and on a whim, I put 2 carrots into the mini food processor and created an Orange Brick Road that I likened to sunburned bodies spread all over the beach. If you go to my video on YouTube or Facebook, you can see that it turned out kinda fun.

APPLE/RAISIN/PECAN ORGASM

I'm a big fan of sugar, that's no secret. But, seriously, sometimes I just have to be kinder to my pancreas. This is sorta the cheat-diet version of a baked apple, but with just a tad of naughty from the honey or maple syrup. Great fiber and super satisfying. We all need satisfaction, right?

INGREDIENTS

1 cup (150 g) raisins

8 fist-sized sweet apples

1 cup (120 g) pecans

SEE CINNAMON-SUGAR CANDIED PECANS, PAGE 69

½ cup (120 ml) real maple syrup or honey

ASSEMBLY AND PREP

Preheat the oven to 350°F (177°C). Grease up a 9 x 9–inch (23 x 23–cm) baking dish. Cover the raisins with warm tap water while you . . .

Peel, core and cut the apples into chunks. Chop the pecans into raisin-sized pieces. Dump the water out of the raisins. Mix the apples, raisins and pecans together in a bowl. Spread it all in the baking dish. Pour the honey or syrup sparingly over the mixture.

Bake COVERED for about 30 minutes.

SERVE IT UP

Yeah, this—in a small bowl, either hot or cold—is divine. Nature's gifts to us are fruits and nuts. Uh, don't go there.

PUMPKIN SPICE HALLOWEEN DIP

I was challenged to bring something gross looking to a Halloween party, so I decided that my classic pumpkin dip would look super gaggable if I added raisins and currants to it—sorta a cross between doggie diarrhea and vomit. It worked. Party-goers passed it up until one brave soul tried it and then passed the whole fucking plate around daring people to try it without telling them what it was. It helped that I had found some little graham crackers that looked like Chihuahua logs.

SERVES 30

INGREDIENTS

2 (8-oz [225-g]) packages cream cheese, softened to room temperature

1 (15-oz [425-g]) can pumpkin

2 cups (260 g) confectioner's sugar, sifted smooth

1 tsp cinnamon

1 tsp ginger

1 tsp pumpkin spice

1 cup (150 g) raisins

OR HALF RAISINS/HALF CURRANTS

1 (16-oz [455-g]) package of gingersnap or graham cookies

ASSEMBLY AND PREP

Using an electric mixer, set on medium, beat the cream cheese and pumpkin until smooth. Fold the sugar into the mix with a spatula or big spoon before turning the beaters back on. Really, don't add the sugar while the beaters are running or you'll have the drug cops all over you.

Fold in the 3 brown spices and mix thoroughly. Remove the beaters and lick if you still know how to be a kid. Fold in the raisins and/or currants and let the dip chill up.

SERVE IT UP

Put the dip into a small, clear bowl in the middle of a suitably-themed Halloween (or fall décor) plate and stack the cookies all around the bowl. If you wanna be really cruel, sprinkle some more raisins around the top of the cookies.

TIP: This easily makes 2 to 3 batches, so you can stretch your party cred by taking a batch to work and maybe another to a Thanksgiving feast with family or friends.

PEPPERMINT BARK COOKIE DIP

Woo-hoo, let's hear it for holiday potlucks. I heard that some smart marketing guru dreamed up this recipe so that you could get everything you needed at your local quick-shop market on the way to a party and not show up looking like a loser. This also puts the pumpkin spice into the closet and replaces it with peppermint. It's a seasonal thing, I guess. Point is, though, that it's fucking yummy and super pretty if you serve it with style. This'll up your partygoer score for sure.

SERVES 24

INGREDIENTS

¼ cup (45 g) crushed red/white peppermint candy canes or mints

⅓ cup (60 g) shaved chocolate bar pieces

1 (4-oz [115-g]) package cream cheese, softened

1 (8-oz [225-g]) container Cool Whip, defrosted

NON-AMERICANS, USE WHIPPING CREAM THAT'S BEEN WELL CHILLED AND IS STIFF.

1 (14-oz [395-g]) package of Oreo cookies

Mini candy canes, optional

ASSEMBLY AND PREP

Smash the peppermint candies in a plastic bag. Beat 'em with a hammer to get the pieces super small. Use a cheese grater or mini food processor to get the chocolate bar pieces super small. Mix the cream cheese and Cool Whip together until blended smooth. Whip that shit to within an inch of its life. You want a few bits of cream cheese to hang out, but not too many.

Fold the peppermint shreds and chocolate bits into the creamy mix and let it chill again. Don't mess with it too much or the pink color will start to run.

SERVE IT UP

Put the dip into a small, clear bowl in the middle of a festive holiday plate and stack the Oreos all around the bowl. Hang a few mini candy canes on the outer edge of the bowl for some cool catering-level holiday fuckery. So delicious and so pretty! Extra points for this if you're a dude.

CINNAMON-SUGAR CANDIED PECANS

Mixing candy and nuts together is about as good as it gets. Well, almost as good as mixing chocolate and fruit and nuts, but you get my drift. These little fuckers are awesomeness on a summer salad, on top of ice cream or just for nibbling. Tied up with a bow in a pretty glass jar, these make a lovely gift any time of year. Homemade rocks!

The only hard part about this is finding parchment paper in the grocery store. It should be by the plastic wrap and aluminum foil. If you can't find it, use a silicone baking sheet on your cookie sheet or you'll be stuck with a miserable fucking mess.

MAKES 1 POUND (455 G)

INGREDIENTS

1 cup (190 g) sugar

2 tsp (5 g) ground cinnamon

1 tsp salt

2 egg whites

2 tbsp (30 ml) water

½ tsp vanilla extract

1 lb (455 g) pecan halves

ASSEMBLY AND PREP

Preheat the oven to 250°F (121°C). Line the cookie sheet with parchment paper. In a large zip-top plastic bag, combine the sugar, cinnamon and salt.

In a big-ass bowl, whisk together the egg whites, water and vanilla. Add the pecans to the bowl and stir so that they get all slimy and coated. Use a slotted spoon and drop them into the plastic bag. Now shake the shit out of 'em so they're coated everywhere. Grab a different clean spoon, dig 'em outta the bag and spread them on the cookie sheet. Try not to let them touch. They need to bake, not reproduce.

Bake for at least an hour, but stir 3 to 4 times.

SERVE IT UP

Once they cool to room temperature, store them in an airtight bag or jar.

HEAVENLY DARK CHOCOLATE BARK

MAKES 2 POUNDS (910 G)

Mixing chocolate, fruit and nuts together is a no-brainer. I just talked about that, right? This gets a little messy cuz it's not all waxed like store-bought chocolates, but you just keep a napkin handy. I took this to a retreat once, and I thought people were gonna strangle me if I didn't give up the recipe. And, just like the pecans, homemade rocks!

INGREDIENTS

1 (6-oz [170-g]) package dried cherries

1 (8-oz [225-g]) small package walnut pieces

2 (12-oz [340-g]) packages semi-sweet chocolate chips

ASSEMBLY AND PREP

For this, you're gonna need a smooth, round bowl that you can sit in a pan of warm water. If you have a double boiler in your pan collection, that will work too.

Cut the dried cherries into small pieces (I used food scissors rather than a knife). Break the walnuts into smallish pieces, but not crumbs. Pour the chocolate chips into the round bowl, and set it in the water. As the chocolate starts to melt, stir in the cherries and nuts. When it's all melted evenly, spread it out on a cookie sheet to cool. When it's cool, break it up by hand into uneven pieces.

SERVE IT UP

Uh, yeah, put it out on the table in a box or a plate or whatever. Serve napkins with it.

Prepare to share the recipe. You'll be mobbed.

FISH IS GOOD FOR YOU

Luckily, for a girl who grew up Catholic on the Atlantic shore in Massachusetts, I LOOOOOOOOVE fish. Everything except swordfish. But I don't like it raw. Sushi or poke aren't for me. After abandoning the cold weather at the age of nineteen, I've lived in Southern California within five miles (8 km) of the Pacific Ocean for 50-plus years, and I still love fish. Whenever I travel, I try local fish. Walleye sandwich in Grand Marais, Minnesota? Oh my goodness. Fresh Mahi-Mahi in Maui? Yes. Copper River salmon grilled quickly and then served on a cedar plank in Redmond, Washington? Hell yes.

I really anguished over which favorite fish recipes to put in this cookbook—I have to keep some secrets, you know. My fave cold dish is the Salmon Surprise Salad (page 74), and my favorite fast hot dish is the Easy Shrimp Gumbo (page 82). OH my goodness . . . the Gumbo! My favorite day-off fish dish is the Shrimp Magique (page 78). Blisstastic! FUCK YEAH!

If you don't like fish, at least try the sauces and preparations with something you do like. Glug glug.

SALMON SURPRISE SALAD

Okay, my secret is fully out now. I'm a freak for fruit—all fruit. Pairing mango and salmon happened by accident for me one day. It was all I had in my fridge and I was fucking starving. I've since served it up for my lady friends on top of a very light orzo salad that I dreamed up. Swoon. This combo has so much going for it: textures, tastes, temperatures.

SERVES 4

INGREDIENTS

¾ cup (150 g) uncooked orzo

1 tbsp (15 ml) olive oil

2 tsp (10 ml) lemon juice

¼ tsp honey

1 cup (150 g) ripe mango, cubed

FROZEN MANGO CUBES WILL WORK JUST AS WELL ONCE YOU THAW THEM.

2 stalks celery, sliced paper thin

1 carrot, sliced paper thin

1 burpless cucumber, sliced thin

½ tsp fresh dill, chopped fine

½ cup (115 g) crumbled goat cheese

1 lb (455 g) fresh salmon steaks

Butter, salt and pepper for sautéing

ASSEMBLE AND COOK

In a big-ass pasta pan, cook (test for doneness at 8 minutes), drain and rinse the orzo. Set it aside in a bowl for a sec to cool.

Back in that same pan, mix together the olive oil, lemon juice and honey. If you had any juice from slicing up your mango, add it now. Just the juice. Stir the cooled orzo into the dressing in the pan to coat it with all the deliciousness. Stir in the celery, carrot, cucumber and dill. Stir in the goat cheese—feta is too strong, trust me.

Salad is done, hang tight. Sauté the salmon in a little butter, salt and pepper until done—maximum 2 minutes per side.

SERVE IT UP

Put the orzo salad into individual bowls, top with a warm piece of salmon each and arrange cooled mango pieces all around the edges. Are you ready to swoon?

TOFISHIN

Not into meat? Like fish? A fan of tofu and veggies? This is just for you. Just like the fried rice dish on page 86, this can be customized if you don't care for any of the ingredients I list.

SERVES 2

INGREDIENTS

½ tsp olive oil

1 small stalk broccoli, chopped

OR FROZEN BROCCOLI FLORETS STRAIGHT FROM FREEZER BAG TO PAN

1 bell pepper, chopped

1 onion, chopped

¼ tsp ground ginger

¼ tsp pepper flakes

1 lb (455 g) mild white fish

SOLE OR TILAPIA WORK GREAT

1 (14-oz [395-g]) block extra firm tofu, cubed right outta the package, no need to press

Soy sauce to taste

ASSEMBLE AND COOK

Heat the oil in a wok-style pan over medium-high heat. Toss in the broccoli, pepper and onion; stir vigorously. Sprinkle in the ginger and pepper flakes so everything is coated evenly. Keep stirring over medium-high heat. This shit cooks fast, 1 to 2 minutes max. Pay attention.

Toss in the fish and it will naturally break up as it gets nearly done. Toss in the tofu cubes just as the fish starts to break up. Depending on the fish you chose, this could be 2 to 4 minutes. Stir vigorously another 2 minutes or so until the tofu is warmed up. That's it, you're done.

SERVE IT UP

Dump that shit into some bowls, and dig in. Sprinkle soy sauce on for a little extra zip. If it's what you like, you'll be thrilled.

SHRIMP MAGIQUE

This is a day-off recipe because of the 2 hours to marinate the shrimp—it's really do-ahead FAST as FUCK, and it's so freakin' delicious that I couldn't finish the cookbook without it. There, you found my weakness: I had to give you my best shit, even if it takes more than 20 minutes to fix.

SERVES 4

INGREDIENTS

1 small onion, chopped

2 cloves garlic, if you like it (I don't)

1 lime, juiced and about 1 tbsp (10 g) of the rind, zested

1 cup (40 g) fresh parsley, chopped

¼ cup (60 ml) olive oil

¼ cup (60 ml) soy sauce

1 lb (455 g) frozen shrimp, medium sized, thawed

8 to 10 aluminum foil sheets, each about 12 x 12 in (30 x 30 cm)

1 zucchini, sliced ¼ inch (0.5 cm) thick

1 yellow crookneck squash, sliced into ¼-inch (0.5-cm) thick pieces

1 red bell pepper, chopped very small

1–2 cups (145–290 g) frozen whole-kernel corn

4 cups (645 g) cooked rice for serving

ASSEMBLY AND PREP

In a blender or food processor, combine the onion, garlic, lime juice and zest, parsley, olive oil and soy sauce; blend until smooth. Place the marinade and shrimp in a zip-top bag and toss it around until everything's covered. Place in the fridge for 2 to 4 hours.

This will work in a toaster oven, a conventional oven, on an outdoor BBQ or even a campfire. Key to success is medium heat, 375°F (190°C) for an oven, glowing for a BBQ or campfire.

Lay the foil sheets out on the counter. Lightly spray each one with cooking spray or grease like you would a baking dish. Put your prepped veggies together in one bowl and your shrimp plucked out of the marinade in another. Dump a big spoonful of each into the center of the foil squares, with the shrimp on top. Gather opposite sides of the foil and join at the top with a fold. Then fold in the edges. A tight seal is important. Put the foil pouches in the oven or on the grill and cook for 10 to 12 minutes.

By this time, the shrimp should be opaque. Open one pouch carefully to check. Don't get a steam burn. I know, that seems complicated, but it's not—really, trust me.

Oh, and if you don't want to fuss with individual foil pouches, put the shit in a pre-greased square glass casserole dish, veggies on the bottom, shrimp on top, covered tightly with foil, and bake at 375°F (190°C) for 25 minutes.

SERVE IT UP

Everybody gets a pouch and a bowl of rice and they're good to go. Crack open a beer and prepare for raves. You earned it. This one is hand-intensive, but so worth it.

FISH IN A DISH

Some days all you have the energy to do is throw three things together and call it supper/dinner/chow, whatever-the-fuck. So, here ya go. THREE THINGS. What makes this work so well on a night when you're beat to shreds is texture: flaky fish, crunchy asparagus spears or smooth, silky zucchini spears and the zing of lemon juice/butter/dill running over it all.

SERVES 2-4

INGREDIENTS

1 bunch (160 g) fresh asparagus or 2 medium-sized zucchini (approx. 390 g)

1 lb (455 g) fish fillets

> *MY FAVORITE IS FRESH SALMON; PICK YOURS.*

Salt and pepper as desired

Some fresh (or dried) dill (Okay, I cheated)

1 lemon

ASSEMBLY AND PREP

Preheat your oven to 400°F (204°C). Grease up your favorite rectangular baking pan or dish. Wash the asparagus or slice the zucchini lengthwise. Line the bottom of the dish with the veggies. Lay the fish, skin-side down, on top of the veggies. Sprinkle salt, pepper and dill on the fish. Slice the lemon and put slices on top of all the fish pieces. Bake it, covered with foil, for 25 minutes.

SERVE IT UP

Grab some crackers or make some toast (or even make some quick-cooking rice while this bakes). Boom, it's time to eat. You're welcome.

What? You hate fish? Well, then try it with boneless chicken pieces. FINE! Go ahead, fuck with my recipe. See if I care.

EASY SHRIMP GUMBO (SAUSAGE OPTIONAL)

SERVES 4

I'm a firm believer that if you cook okra until it no longer looks like snot, it's tasty and makes a fine fucking gumbo. You can throw this tasty dish together in a fast few minutes and put a hot steaming bowl of awesome on the table. A clever combo of fresh, canned and frozen shit is your secret here. It does take two pans, so lay them out first. A wok-ish pan and a pasta-sized pan.

INGREDIENTS

2 lbs (0.9 kg) fresh okra, cut into ¼-inch (0.5-cm) slices

2 fist-sized onions, chopped

1 tbsp (15 ml) olive oil

2 (35-oz [990-g]) cans chopped/crushed tomatoes

1 (16-oz [455-g]) can whole-kernel corn

1 (8-oz [225-g]) package frozen baby lima beans

1 tsp salt

½ tsp pepper

¼ tsp ground thyme

¼ tsp cayenne pepper, if you like it hot

1–2 tbsp (15–30 ml) Worcestershire sauce, depending on your taste

4 cups (650 g) white rice

1 lb (455 g) medium pre-cooked shrimp

1 (13-oz [360-g]) package andouille sausage, or Hillshire Farms sausage if you can't find andouille, optional

ASSEMBLE AND COOK

Cook the okra and onions in the oil over medium-high heat until you can begin to see through the onion, about 5 minutes. The slimy part of the okra should be cooking out by now. Keep stirring until the juicy slime disappears.

Combine the tomatoes, corn, limas, seasonings and Worcestershire sauce into the big, pasta-sized pan on medium-low heat. Stir to make sure nothing feels neglected. Now add the onion/okra mix. Simmer uncovered for about 30 to 45 minutes.

Cook up some rice and start a load of laundry or catch up on social media. When the rice is about done, add the shrimp to the gumbo. You can also add the sausage if you want to go full New Orleans on its ass. The shrimp and/or sausage are already precooked, so all you need to do is heat them to the same temp as the gumbo, maybe 5 minutes.

SERVE IT UP

Lay out 4 wide, shallow bowls and 4 mouth-sized spoons. Scoop some rice into each bowl. Ladle some gumbo over the rice. Add hot sauce or whatever floats your boat. Yummmmmmmmy. Go for it.

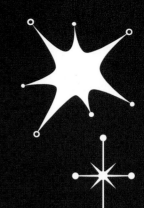

COMFORTING CASSEROLES & ONE-POT LIFESAVERS

Casseroles and one-pot meals are the non-runny version of soup: if you like it, it goes in. If not, fuck it! These are stress-inducing for people who don't like their food to touch, so if you're one of them, skip ahead. If you're less concerned about your food touching but someone in your family is, then make these and you'll get to enjoy them all by yourself. Welcome to Leftover City—the number one reason to make casseroles and one-pot dishes. I've given you lots of ideas here, and I'm sure you can throw in ucky shit you like that I don't like—onions and garlic, for example. Pour on hot sauce or go hog wild with the jalapeños. Do what feels good. It's your belly.

FAST AS FUCK FRIED RICE

SERVES 5–7

I'm a rice fanatic. It's so fucking versatile. You can mix it into a casserole, stretch leftovers for one more meal, make it into dessert, or it can be the base ingredient for a made-your-way-at-home fried rice that includes only the shit you like. Hi YA!

INGREDIENTS

2 tbsp (30 ml) olive oil or vegetable oil

1 cup (235 ml) each of your 5 favorite ingredients, chopped up small (my favorites are peas, pea pods, shrimp, zucchini and broccoli)

THAT'S 5 CUPS (1.2 L) OF GOOD SHIT IF YOU COUNTED CORRECTLY. IF YOU PUT IN MORE THAN 5 INGREDIENTS, YOU'LL NEED MORE RICE.

Dried pepper flakes, if you like 'em

2 cups (320 g) already-cooked rice

DO NOT USE RICE IN A BAG; THAT SHIT'S NASTY AND CLUMPY AND NOT WORTH YOUR TIME OR $$.

Soy sauce to taste, or whatever Asian seasoning you like best

1 cup (150 g) maximum of pineapple tidbits for the very last

OPTIONAL

Onions, scrambled egg, bell pepper, carrots, bean sprouts, whatever

ASSEMBLE AND COOK

Turn the heat up high and get the oil hot to trot. Test by dropping in one tiny piece of the chopped ingredients. Just one piece, dearie.

When the oil starts to sputter, throw in the rest of the chopped ingredients and give 'em a hot sauté. You want this shit to be cooked and warm—not still raw, but not mushy. If you like pepper flakes, throw 'em in while this shit cooks. Probably won't take more than 4 to 5 minutes if you chopped your shit small enough. Dump the sautéed chopped shit into a separate bowl to stand by for a little bit.

Now throw the already-cooked rice into the empty wok and stir until it starts to get some color. Watch carefully. Stir faster so it doesn't stick to the bottom of the pan. Color is good. Burned is fucked. Stand at the stove and stir. Watch it carefully; the heat is still on high. Maybe 4 to 5 minutes. Once your rice has the color you want, lightly sprinkle soy sauce (or teriyaki sauce if you like that better), but no clumps; stir vigorously to mix the soy sauce in thoroughly.

FINAL ASSEMBLY

Dump the cooked veggies and meats back into the wok with the rice and stir around for maybe 3 to 5 minutes. Stir all the time and keep the heat up. Just when you think it's done, pour in the pineapple (if you like it). Stir it around for another minute.

SERVE IT UP

Ladle it right out of the wok into individual bowls. If you're dexterous, use chopsticks. Most yummy.

SLOP

I have a bad case of the guilts calling this a recipe—it's merely cooking pasta, frying some meat, opening a bunch of cans and throwing together shit that gets along. Like a hookup but with no drunk texts. It's an adaptation of the only gross POS my mother ever made. Once I grew up and had my own family to feed, I included only the shit that I like and that they would eat. My ex is the one who named it SLOP. This tastes okay right after you make it, but the bomb is Day 2 or Day 3—make enough for leftovers or you'll hate yourself.

8-10 SERVINGS

● ●

INGREDIENTS

2 lbs (0.9 kg) ground beef

➤ *DON'T GO CHEAP; BUY THE LOW FAT.*

2 cups (230 g) of your favorite medium-sized pasta (elbows, rotini, etc.)

➤ *UNDERCOOK AND COOK THE NIGHT BEFORE TO SAVE TIME ON MEAL DAY.*

1 tbsp (15 g) butter

1 (16 oz [455 g]) can whole-kernel corn

1 (16-oz [455-g]) can French-style green beans

1 (16-oz [455-g]) can tomato sauce, my favorite is Hunt's (more if you like it juicy)

1 (32-oz [905-g]) can chopped or puréed tomatoes (your choice)

1 (10-oz [285-g]) can mushroom tips and stems, if your fam likes 'em

1 (4-oz [115-g]) can chopped olives, if your fam likes 'em

1 tbsp (15 ml) Worcestershire sauce

1 tbsp (15 ml) steak sauce, such as A-1

1 tbsp (12 g) sugar

➤ *YES, SUGAR*

¼ cup (45 g) Parmesan cheese to sprinkle on each serving

Salt, pepper to taste

ASSEMBLE AND COOK

Fry the ground meat and separate while frying. You want crumbles, not meatballs. Size matters. Set aside.

A big-ass pan is your best friend for this dish. Cook the pasta in it, leaving it still a little chewy—don't let it get mushy. Drain and then stir a little bit of butter into it to keep it from sticking together. In a big-ass bowl, combine all the other ingredients except the Parmesan, salt and pepper—EVERYTHING at once.

Now, using either the big pan or the big bowl, combine the meat/veg/sauce shit with the pasta and stir. Heat it up again, either by single servings or nuke enough to feed whoever is at the table waiting.

SERVE IT UP

Serve it up in shallow bowls. Sprinkle liberally with shredded Parmesan cheese. Salt and pepper to taste. Add spicy shit if you wish, like sautéed onions and/or bell peppers, hot sauce, pepper flakes and a dab of chili powder—but don't go crazy.

ENCHILADA CASSEROLE

Super fast, super delicious, super easy—and it's Mexican food, which is always a winner. Make rolled enchiladas or layer this shit; either way, prepare for nirvana. This is amazing as soon as you make it, and gets better each time you reheat it. I'm a fool for leftovers, I admit it. How else do you get FAST as FUCK two nights in a row?

SERVES 6-8

INGREDIENTS

1 (32-oz [905-g]) can red enchilada sauce

12 corn tortillas

1 lb (455 g) cooked ground meat—your choice

➤ DON'T GO CHEAP, BUY THE LOW FAT.

or 1 lb (455 g) chopped/sautéed vegetables such as onions, bell peppers, carrots and potatoes

➤ CHOP INTO VERY SMALL CUBES (BLUEBERRY-SIZED).

1 (8-oz [225-g]) package Mexican-blend shredded cheese

1 (4-oz [115-g]) can chopped olives, optional if your fam likes 'em

OPTIONAL GARNISHES

Jalapeños

Sour cream

ASSEMBLE AND COOK

Set out a rectangular glass casserole dish and put your ingredients in a circle around it in separate bowls. No need to grease it up. Put the enchilada sauce in a shallow bowl big enough that you can dip the tortillas into it.

Dip a corn tortilla so it's covered on both sides and place in the casserole dish. Grab 2 tablespoons (30 g) of the meat or veggies, spoon 1 tablespoon (15 g) of cheese and spread to the edges. Add some olives if you want and roll the tortilla up. Repeat until the ingredients are used up and the casserole dish is full. Feel free to squeeze the enchiladas together. If you want to make a layered casserole instead, dip the tortillas in the sauce and make a layer of tortillas in the pan, followed by the meat/veggies, followed by the cheese. Repeat until you've used up everything.

Heat uncovered in a 300°F (150°C) oven for 30 minutes, or until the sauce bubbles. Top with jalapeños and sour cream if that's your thing.

TIP: Leftover chicken, pork or turkey will save cooking time. YUM.

PIZZA BURGER CASSEROLE

SERVES 6-8 (IF THEY'RE NOT TEENAGERS)

Do you or your kids clamor for pizza five nights a week? That can get pricey, it can be way too loaded with fat and sodium and you can get stuck in a rut. Who needs that? Here's an alternative that tastes just as good—and you can make it your way.

INGREDIENTS

2 lb (0.9 kg) hamburger or ground turkey

¼ onion, chopped

→ IF YOU LIKE THAT SHIT

Pinch each of: salt, Italian seasoning and pepper flakes

→ IF YOU LIKE 'EM

1 can of 8 refrigerated buttermilk biscuits

1 (8-oz [225-g]) can tomato sauce

1 (4-oz [115-g]) can sliced mushrooms, drained

1 (4-oz [115-g]) can diced black olives, drained

1 (15-oz [425 g]) can diced tomatoes

1 (8-oz [225-g]) package shredded pizza-blend cheese

ASSEMBLE AND COOK

In a large skillet, brown the ground meat until no juice remains (and sauté the onions if you like 'em). Add the salt, Italian seasoning and pepper flakes.

Preheat the oven to whatever temperature is on your package of biscuits. Grease a 9 x 12–inch (23 x 30–cm) baking dish; then press the biscuits into the bottom of the dish. Spread 'em out so that they touch and there's no holes in what is essentially the bottom crust of this fuckin' masterpiece. Spread the tomato sauce over the biscuits in an even layer.

Combine the hamburger, mushrooms, black olives and tomatoes. Then spoon or pour it over the biscuit mix. Be gentle. Top that amazing mess by covering it with the pizza blend cheese.

Bake at the oven temperature shown on the biscuit can. Bake for 5 to 10 minutes longer than the can says, or until the biscuits are cooked through. (Be careful not to burn the bottom of the biscuits! You want to eat this, not use it for a weapon.)

SERVE IT UP

Let it sit still on the counter for about 8 minutes after you take it out of the oven. This'll give you time to corral your hungry mob and get 'em to wash up before dinner. No dirty hands at the table, and no fuckin' cell phones either.

Cut fancy shapes and chow down. Hope for leftovers. Stretch it by serving a salad or some broccoli alongside it. I mean, pizza and broccoli is a natural match, right? Like pineapple.

NOTE: Half a cup (110 g) of pepperoni, Canadian bacon or cooked sausage can be added to the ground meat if you want to spike the sodium count and zing the flavor meter! Oh, and pineapple!

CHICKEN, RICE AND PEAS

My family knows I'm reverting to ten years old when I put this on the table. I've also been known to cheat by buying a precooked chicken, cooking the rice separately, then adding the peas and gravy (no can juice and no soup) and serving it alongside the precooked chicken pulled apart. Whatever works for you when you're in a hurry is fine with me. I won't tell a soul.

SERVES 2-4

INGREDIENTS

1 cup (210 g) uncooked quick-cooking rice

1 (15-oz [425-g]) can tiny peas

1 (12-oz [340 g]) jar chicken gravy

1 (11-oz [310-g]) can cream of celery soup

1 lb (455 g) boneless chicken pieces

BREASTS OR THIGHS, YOUR CHOICE

½ tsp poultry seasoning

Salt and pepper, to your liking

ASSEMBLY AND PREP

Preheat the oven to 325°F (163°C). Grease up a 9 x 13–inch (23 x 33–cm) casserole dish.

Mix the rice, peas (and can juice), gravy and soup together in a bowl. Add half a soup can of water. Spread that mix in the dish. Lay the whole uncooked chicken pieces in a single layer on top of the rice/peas mixture. Sprinkle lightly with poultry seasoning, salt and pepper.

Bake covered for 35 to 40 minutes. Remove the foil or pan cover and brown for another 10 minutes. Add a little water if it looks like it needs it.

SERVE IT UP

This is pretty easy. Dish it outta the casserole pan and put it on plates. Wheeee.

HURRY UP BEEF STROGANOFF

When you long to have Julia Child show up in your kitchen and make you something rich and delicious but know full well that she can't/won't, this'll do. It's amazing how fucking good this tastes when you realize you made it with frickin' hamburger meat. Some days, you just get to shine. Today's your day.

SERVES 2-4

● ●

INGREDIENTS

2 cups (180 g) uncooked egg noodles

1 lb (455 g) very lean ground beef

8–10 fresh garden variety white mushrooms

➤ *OR EVEN CANNED WILL DO*

1 stalk green onions, chopped fine

⅛ tsp garlic salt

1 (10.5-oz [300-g]) can cream of mushroom soup

1 cup (120 g) sour cream

➤ *CREAM CHEESE WILL DO IN A PINCH*

ASSEMBLE AND COOK

In pan #1, boil water and start cooking the noodles; cook until just tender. At 8 to 10 minutes, do the chew test—if they're a little chewy, they're almost there.

Meanwhile, in a frying pan (#2) on medium-high heat, brown the beef. Drain and put in a bowl for a quick minute. Sauté the mushrooms and green onions in the remaining beef juice with the garlic salt, 4 to 5 minutes until barely warmed. Return the beef to the frying pan. Add the soup and sour cream to pan #2, and stir gently on low heat.

Cover the beef/soup pan and turn heat to low while the noodles finish cooking. This time when you do the chew test, it should be perfect. Total time: 10 to 12 minutes.

Drain the noodles and put them back in pan #1. Pour the stroganoff mixture over top and stir to mix thoroughly.

SERVE IT UP

If you have time, throw some frozen peas into a pan so you can serve them alongside a helping of this quick and easy fake-it-til-you-taste-it stroganoff. It'll fill your belly with yumness. The peas just add color for a nice presentation. A salad would do the same thing. YAY, you.

VEGGING OUT

I'm a big fan of vegetables—always have been, ever since my parents had a backyard garden when I was six or seven. Man-oh-man, fresh carrots washed and chomped into three minutes after being pulled from the ground? Asparagus steamed within an hour of being cut from the plant, slathered with butter, stacked on crispy buttered toast? Oh. My. Tastegasmic. Goodness.

Yeah, I know, once I moved to southern California, some angel introduced me to avocado—creamy, nutty, versatile, goes-with-everything, stuff-it-spread-it-slather-it, de-fucking-licious avocado. Who needs anything else, except that if you have your own tree, they all come ripe at the same time and you've gotta scramble to give 'em away. Same with a zucchini plant. It's remarkably fertile. Thank you, bees.

A few local growers where I live have fresh veggies even though they're bigger farms, so I indulge whenever I can. Vine-ripened, plump juicy tomatoes, yellow crookneck squash and fresh baby asparagus are highlights for me. Sweet corn in season sends me into a state of grace. If you grow your own, I salute you.

VEGGIE LOAF MUFFINS

This was an on-camera experiment to make a meatloaf alternative for a good friend who is vegetarian. Because he doesn't throw a fit at eggs or Worcestershire sauce, I used the same binding goop that I use for meatballs. He was thrilled with the results and I've since made it for other friends who say it's lit. The grab-and-go aspect of making muffins instead of a loaf meant that they cooked faster than a dense loaf shape. They also really worked well for busting them out one at a time for his lunch box.

MAKES 10–12

INGREDIENTS

1 cello pack of saltine crackers

OR

1 cup (160 g) cooked brown rice for GF reasons

3 large eggs

¾ cup (175 ml) ketchup

1 tsp brown mustard

OR YELLOW IF YOU MUST

1 tbsp (15 ml) Worcestershire sauce

3 tbsp (45 ml) steak sauce, such as A-1

1 cup (125 g) zucchini, chopped

1 cup (125 g) yellow squash, chopped

1 medium onion, chopped small

1 bunch (340 g) fresh spinach, rinsed and chopped

½ cup (40 g) fresh mushrooms, chopped

1 (16-oz [455-g]) can lentils

1 (16-oz [455-g]) can black beans

ASSEMBLY AND PREP

Preheat the oven to 325°F (163°C). Line a muffin pan with cupcake papers.

Put the whole cello pack of saltines into a large plastic bag and smash into tiny crumbs. In a medium bowl, crack the eggs and add the liquid ingredients. Whisk well. Now add the crumbs (or the rice) to the liquid mush and let it sit for a tiny bit.

In another bowl, mix the raw veggies with the beans—knead and squish through your fingers. Use a potato masher if it seems like shit needs to get cozier.

Now, mix in the crumbs/liquid paste and work it thoroughly into the veggie/bean mixture. Fill the cupcake papers nearly to the top. Bake for about 40 minutes. You're really only warming this shit up and slightly cooking the veggies.

SERVE IT UP

Veggie muffins for din din—with a salad, yummy.

NOTE: If you don't have cupcake papers, be SURE to grease the cupcake holes very well.

This shit WILL stick to the edges. Also, don't try to make a loaf out of this. It doesn't hold together well. Muffins are the ticket.

EGGPLANT ZUCCHINI BLISS

SERVES 6-8

Prepare for veggie-gasm with this totally green yumness. Low carb, too.

• •

INGREDIENTS

1 medium eggplant, diced to walnut size

1 medium zucchini, diced a little smaller

2 tbsp (30 ml) olive oil

1 small bunch fresh baby spinach (about 10 oz [220 g])

½ cup (120 ml) water

1½ cups (355 ml) spaghetti sauce (page 29) without adding the meat

➤ *YOU DID FREEZE SOME, RIGHT?*

1½ cups (180 g) shredded pizza-cheese mix

➤ *OR VEGAN CHEESE IF YOU WISH*

Pasta or rice for serving, optional

ASSEMBLY AND PREP

Preheat the oven to 375°F (190°C) and grease up a 9 x 13–inch (23 x 33–cm) glass casserole dish.

In a deep skillet or wok, with the heat at medium, cook the eggplant and zucchini in the olive oil until just barely softened and beginning to brown, about 5 minutes. Now throw in the baby spinach and the ½ cup (120 ml) of water, but be careful you don't get a steam burn. Cover and let it simmer for about 3 to 4 minutes. Smelling yummy yet?

Add in the spaghetti sauce and stir well, so that everything is coated. Now, pour it into the casserole dish and spread the cheese all over the top. Bake until the cheese is fully melted, maybe 12 to 15 minutes or so.

SERVE IT UP

Pull it outta the oven and let it cool for 5 minutes or so: veggie wondrousness for you. Serve with pasta or rice if you wish. That sauce from page 29, remember? Sprinkle a little more cheese if you are craving it.

UNSTUFFED ZUCCHINI

How many times has your green-thumb neighbor tried to pawn off the overabundance of squash from her backyard harvest? But who the fuck has time to make a fancy stuffed squash casserole? And, since this shit grows in the summer, who wants to turn on the oven and burn up just to make dinner? Dice, fry and season that shit, then toss it in a big pan or a wok for all the same yummy flavor with one-fourth the work. It all goes in the same piehole, right?

SERVES 2-4

INGREDIENTS

1 each of banana-sized zucchini and yellow squash, chopped into very small cubes (blueberry-sized)

➤ *SIZE MATTERS—SMALL WILL COOK FASTER AND BLEND BETTER.*

Butter or olive oil for sautéing

½ lb (225 g) cooked ground meat (your choice)

➤ *FRY THE GROUND MEAT AND SEPARATE WHILE FRYING. YOU WANT CRUMBLES, NOT MEATBALLS.*

1 (6-oz [170-g]) package rice/wild rice mixture with seasonings, cooked as directed

➤ *USE LESS SEASONING IF WATCHING SODIUM. COOK THE NIGHT BEFORE TO SAVE TIME ON MEAL DAY.*

2 large tomatoes or a combo of multi-colored cherry tomatoes, chopped very small or put in blender or food processor

➤ *SIZE MATTERS. IDEALLY YOU WANT A CHUNKY RELISH RATHER THAN DISCERNIBLE BITS OF TOMATO.*

Shredded Parmesan cheese to taste

Salt and pepper to taste

Pepper flakes, optional

ASSEMBLE AND COOK

In a wok or large nonstick pan, add the chopped zucchini and squash and some butter or olive oil. Sauté until just barely translucent, about 5 minutes. Add the cooked ground meat to the squash. Add the cooked rice to the mix. Add the tomato relish to the mix. Stir, lower the heat and cover for 3 to 4 minutes to make sure everything is uniformly warm.

SERVE IT UP

Serve it up in two shallow bowls. Sprinkle liberally with shredded Parmesan cheese. Add salt and pepper, along with pepper flakes if you wish.

SUBSTITUTIONS

Quinoa or brown rice or wild rice will add texture and crunch (and will increase the prep time).

BONUS: No hot oven, no digging out the center of the squash to play pat-a-cake. Tastes the same.

BUTTERNUT SQUASH AND APPLE ORGASM

Butternut squash by itself is gag-inducing to me—a throwback to baby food, maybe. But a few Thanksgivings ago I put some of this on my plate in an effort to be gracious to my grandson's girlfriend who was bursting with pride at having cooked something more damn difficult than hard-boiled eggs. Oh my FUCKING goodness, was I surprised! This tickled my taste buds and did not make me gag, and actually had me digging for seconds. Rock your Thanksgiving or any fall potluck with this masterpiece.

• •

MAIN INGREDIENTS

2½ Granny Smith apples, peeled and cubed (about 4 cups [720 g])

½ butternut squash, peeled and cubed (about 2½ cups [390 g])

➤ *BAKE THAT SUCKER FOR ABOUT 30 MINUTES AT 300°F (150°C) BEFORE YOU TRY TO PEEL IT.*

¼–½ cup (35–70 g) brown sugar

➤ *DON'T OVERDO IT—SUPPLEMENTS THE TART/SWEET OF THE APPLES.*

2 tsp (5 g) cinnamon

1 (4-oz [115-g]) packet of dried cranberries, craisins or currants, optional

¼ cup (60 ml) water

TOPPING INGREDIENTS

1 cup (125 g) all-purpose flour

¼–½ cup (35–70 g) brown sugar

½ tbsp (4 g) pumpkin pie spice

1 tsp cinnamon—yes, just a pinch more; it's good for you

⅓–½ cup (75–115 g) butter

½ cup (60 g) chopped walnuts or pecans

ASSEMBLE AND COOK

Preheat the oven to 400°F (204°C).

In a big-ass bowl, toss the apples and squash with the brown sugar and 2 teaspoons (5 g) of cinnamon. Sprinkle in the dried fruit if you like that shit. Pour into a baking dish, sprinkle the water over the top to baptize it and bake, covered, for 20 minutes.

While that shit is heating up, wash your big-ass bowl, and then use it to combine the flour, brown sugar, pumpkin spice and more cinnamon. Mix with a big fork. Add the butter and mix it some more, but not too well—let it stay clumpy.

Take the heated-up apple-squash mix out of the oven, and then evenly spread the crumble over top of it. Smelling orgasmic, right? Spread some chopped nuts on top and bake for an additional 20 minutes, uncovered, or until lightly browned and crispy on top.

SERVE IT UP

Dig into that shit and watch your guests go orgasmic over it.

MEXICAN SWEET POTATO

It turns out that this yummy shit is vegan—who knew? You can add meat and dairy to it if you wish, but this is madly satisfying on its own. Trust me.

INGREDIENTS

2 sweet potatoes

EACH ONE WILL SERVE TWO PEOPLE

¼ tsp chipotle chili powder

¼ tsp paprika

¼ tsp cumin

1 (12-oz [340-g]) bag frozen whole kernel corn

½ tsp olive oil

1 (15-oz [425-g]) can black beans

1 cup (30 g) chopped fresh spinach

¼ cup (10 g) chopped cilantro

½ cup (120 g) of your favorite salsa

1 lime to juice

1 ripe avocado

Sour cream and cotija cheese, optional

ASSEMBLY AND PREP

Bake the sweet potatoes in foil. It usually takes about an hour at 350°F (177°C). Mix the 3 dry seasonings together in a small bowl. Trust me on this one.

Now start on the filling. This calls for a big iron skillet, Mexican style. You do have one, right?

On high heat, brown half the bag of corn kernels in the olive oil. Stir constantly. Browned is good. Burned is fucked. About 3 to 4 minutes should do it. Turn the heat down to medium. Add the beans and seasonings. Stir until it's all warm and smelling orgasmic. Add the spinach and cilantro until the shit just barely wilts. Throw that whole mess into a mixing bowl; then add the salsa and lime juice, and stir.

SERVE IT UP

Cut each potato in quarters. Chop but don't mash. Pour the filling on top. Lay slices of fresh avocado on top for a lovely presentation.

If you want to blow the vegan prep, add sour cream or crumbled cotija cheese to the top.

Olé!

FARFALLE PASTA CARNIVAL

The big key to making this work is using small-shaped pasta: Farfalle is my favorite because there is enough surface for the avocado/tomato mush to stick to. Shells or elbows or pinwheels will work okay, but there's always the chance to fuck it up. And, besides, farfalle just sounds like a carnival, right?

Why sweet potato? Because it's unexpected. You need a better reason? Oh, and if you can't find very ripe tomatoes, use a can of crushed tomatoes. I won't tell.

SERVES 4–6

• •

SPREAD

2 tbsp (30 ml) olive oil

¼ tsp Italian seasoning

1 tsp salt

1 tsp black pepper

1 bunch (1⅓ cups [55 g]) parsley, chopped fine

1 very ripe avocado

4–6 very ripe fresh tomatoes

PASTA INGREDIENTS

1 cup (115 g) uncooked small-shape pasta

2 tbsp (30 ml) olive oil

1 cup (90 g) broccoli florets, chopped

1 cup (150 g) bell pepper, any color, chopped

1 cup (125 g) zucchini or yellow squash, chopped

1 bunch (340 g) fresh spinach, washed and chopped

1 yellow onion, chopped small

1 cup (200 g) cooked sweet potato, chunked

1 (5.5-oz [165-ml]) can V-8 juice, if needed

ASSEMBLY AND PREP

In a small bowl, mix the olive oil, Italian seasoning, salt, pepper and parsley. Mash up the avocado. Core the ripe tomatoes and put them in a blender or food processor, or chop teensy. Add the tomatoes and the olive oil/seasoning mix to the avocados.

In a large saucepan, cook the pasta in 3 cups (720 ml) of the water to your desired tenderness. While the pasta is cooking, sauté the fresh vegetables in olive oil over medium-high heat until crisp and tender, about 5 minutes. Once the veggies and pasta are done, throw 'em in a big bowl and add the chopped-up sweet potato.

Smear the whole thing with the avocado/tomato spread. Now is the time to decide if you need a little shot of the V-8 juice to moisten the whole gorgeous bowl of yumness.

SERVE IT UP

Serve in bowls so that none of the mush escapes. Serve with rounds of French bread for cleaning the bottom of the bowl. It's easier than watching people stick their faces in the bowl to lick it.

SAILING SOLO

Let's look at the best part of cooking for one. You don't have to reach a consensus with ANYONE—you just have to make up your own mind what you want to eat and do it. The pantry/leftovers approach is your golden ticket to eating better food for less money, which will leave you money to do shit like go to the movies or a concert or . . . well, I really don't need to spell that out for you.

Setting aside a little extra time on one day will save you time the next day . . . or two . . . or three. You can do this without wasting food—use the ingredient lists in each recipe to plan your week. Then, if you get to about day four and you're tired of what you cooked and want a change, freeze that shit. Splurge on takeout or grab something out of the freezer that you cooked last month. See, you can do this.

I'm hoping that you've read through the other recipes in this cookbook, taking note of which ones will make awesome meals-for-a-week if you're living in solo bliss. Have you noticed a trend of which foods work really well together and which ones I've avoided? It's chemistry, kids, but don't let that scare you. We're more than halfway through the book, and surely you've figured out that my best advice is to let your imagination run wild and tell your inner critic to STFU.

BUILD-A-PIZZA—PERSONALIZE THAT SHIT

Pizza-for-one is an easy just-got-home-from-work-and-I'm-starving thing to fix. Anything in the fridge or cupboard is fair game. So many options for a base using bread (or not) and so many options for sauces and toppings. Seriously, let your mind go wild. I've seen a veggie restaurant make a base using cauliflower "rice," then slather that shit with pesto sauce, then top it with beets and mushrooms, and finally sprinkle it with fake cheese. At $19 each, it better taste gourmet; that's all I'm saying.

MAKES 2 SLICES

BONUS: One of the funnest dinner parties I ever threw was a make-your-own pizza buffet. I had some bases and sauces ready and asked guests to bring something they really liked—they went fucking nuts. And NOTHING ended up in the trash. Even the veggies and gluten-avoiders were happy.

BASE CHOICES

Boboli® bread

Naan bread

Stale bread cubes pressed into a pan

Cooked rice pressed into a pan

Cauliflower "rice" pressed into a pan

SAUCE CHOICES

1 defrosted cube of your own spaghetti sauce (page 29)

Pesto sauce

Alfredo sauce

Olive oil and salt only

TOPPING CHOICES

Any pre-cooked meat you wish

Any fruit you wish

YES, FRUIT—YOU HEARD ME

Any veggie you wish, pre-cooked unless it's chopped very small

Any legume or leftover you really, really like

Any hot shit you like—if you like it hot, that is

Any cheese you wish, real or not

ASSEMBLY AND PREP

Preheat the oven or toaster oven to 375°F (190°C). Spread sauce on the base of your choice. Sprinkle the toppings liberally, but don't weigh down the base. Bake it in the oven until it's too hot to touch but not too hot to eat. Depending on what you put on it, this could take from 10 to 20 minutes.

Tee hee, you didn't think I'd leave you here, did you? Having to make your own choices? Try these two weird ones. They're super fun and surprisingly delicious.

(continued)

PURPLE VEGGIE PIZZA

I never would have thought of making a pizza base out of cauliflower if I hadn't accompanied one of my pals to a vegan restaurant. I'm like, what the fuck? You call that pizza? Yup, they did, and I had a taste of it 'cuz she dared me. Not too bad—not my first choice, but truly, not too bad. I might even order this shit again. I do love beets. I mean, who doesn't, right? I added goat cheese to my recipe 'cuz the flavor worked like magic with the strong cauliflower and the sweet fresh beets. If you're vegan, you can use something else and we'll all be happy.

MAKES 2 SLICES

INGREDIENTS

1 head cauliflower, steamed until it's mush, about 30 minutes

3 purple beets, steamed, same as the cauliflower

1 bunch (10 cups [340 g]) fresh spinach, steamed for only 1 minute

1 (4-oz [115-g]) container goat cheese

ASSEMBLY AND PREP

Preheat the oven to 375°F (190°C).

After the cauliflower is mush, drain it and then spread it around the bottom of a pizza pan. Peel and chop the beets after they're mush, and layer them over the cauliflower. Lay the spinach leaves over the beets. Sprinkle the goat cheese on top of the spinach. Pop it in the oven for 10 minutes to get it warm again.

SERVE IT UP

Grab a big-ass knife, slice that sucker into manageable pieces and chow down.

BUILD-A-PIZZA—PERSONALIZE THAT SHIT (CONTINUED)

RICE IS NICE DEEP-DISH PIZZA

This amazing combo came to me one day when I had no bread in the house, but I did have a small serving of leftover cooked rice. I spread that shit in a small baking pan and threw some other leftovers on it and called it pizza. DAYUM, kids, it was the bomb. Really light, really refreshing, and you gotta admit that a pesto/chicken combo is always a winner. Seriously, use your imagination anytime you find leftover bits in the fridge. If you like it, that's all that matters. You just might find some magical combo that you can serve at a party and impress the fuck outta your guests.

MAKES 2
SLICES

INGREDIENTS

2 cups (320 g) cooked white or brown rice

½ cup (120 g) pesto sauce

1 cup (230 g) cooked chicken, cut into walnut-sized pieces

½ cup (65 g) mozzarella cheese

ASSEMBLY AND PREP

Preheat the oven to 375°F (190°C). Smash the rice into the bottom and sides of a rectangular casserole dish. Spread a ¼-inch (0.5-cm) layer of pesto sauce over the rice. Sprinkle the chicken over the pesto sauce. Sprinkle the cheese over the chicken. Heat the pizza for 20 minutes, cut into squares and serve.

MAGICAL RICE BOWL

There are pop-up Asian restaurants on every corner, and they'll all have some variation of a rice bowl on the menu. But sometimes you just want to fix it yourself using the shit you like and/or using up leftovers before you have to throw 'em out. This is just the thing. Never had mandarin oranges in your bowl before? Oh, yes you have. It's orange chicken, but with more texture and less fat.

**MAKE IT.
EAT IT.
1 SERVING.**

INGREDIENTS

½ cup (105 g) quick-cooking rice

BROWN OR WHITE

1 cup (185 g) frozen broccoli pieces

1 cup (230 g) leftover chicken meat or steak

½ cup (80 g) shelled edamame or snow peas

1 (4-oz [115-g]) snack pack mandarin oranges, drained

1 tbsp (15 ml) teriyaki sauce, divided

ASSEMBLE AND COOK

Prepare the rice according to directions. While it cooks, heat the broccoli and meat together in a separate small pan. When the broccoli and meat are about done, after 10 minutes, throw in the edamame and oranges. Now add half the teriyaki sauce to the pan and stir quickly.

SERVE IT UP

Dump the cooked rice into a large bowl. Pour the meat/broccoli/edamame/oranges mixture on top of the rice. Add extra teriyaki sauce until it tastes just right.

Grab chopsticks or a spoon, and dig in. Yumness!

LENTIL MUSH IN LETTUCE CUPS

Step right up! Get your legumes. Lovely lentils lazing in lettuce leaves, ready to serve in about 35 minutes. Cheap and filling, good for you, sure to keep you regular and easy on your budget. Come one, come all. Come and get it. Vegan compliant. You sold yet?

SERVES 2 WITH LEFTOVERS

INGREDIENTS

1 cup (200 g) red lentils

2 cups (475 ml) water

1 head iceberg lettuce or butter lettuce, leaves separated, rinsed and dried

1½ cups (150 g) celery, chopped small

1 cup (120 g) fresh carrots, sliced thin

1½ tbsp (45 ml) olive oil

¼ tsp garlic powder

¼ tsp ground ginger

2 tbsp (30 ml) hoisin sauce, if you like it

2 tbsp (30 ml) soy sauce, or less if you're not keen on it

1½ tbsp (22 ml) rice vinegar

1 tsp sesame oil

½ cup (60 g) bean sprouts, if you like 'em

1 (8-oz [225-g]) can water chestnuts, drained and chopped

½ cup (55 g) chopped cashews

1 tbsp (9 g) sesame seeds

ASSEMBLE AND COOK

Pick through the lentils and throw out the boogers. Then rinse them.

Simmer the clean lentils in the water over medium heat for about 15 minutes until just tender. Drain and set aside to cool slightly. While that simmers, break up your lettuce. Wash, pat dry and make some cute little cups. It's smart to double up on the lettuce leaves so the shit won't fall through. Lay 'em out on your plate.

Sauté the celery and carrots with the olive oil in a big skillet until softened, maybe 5 to 6 minutes. Add in the dry spices and sauté about 1 minute longer. The carrots will probably still be crispy. Add in the drained lentils, hoisin sauce, soy sauce, rice vinegar, sesame oil, bean sprouts and water chestnuts. Keep stirring.

Do your best wok tossing (so that nothing sticks) for about another minute. If it starts to look too dry and crumbly, add some water, a tablespoon (15 ml) at a time. Toss in the cashews and sesame seeds at the last minute. Add a tad more water if necessary.

SERVE IT UP

Let the mush cool for just 4 to 5 minutes and then spoon into the lettuce cups. Depending on your appetite, 3 to 5 wraps are just perfect for your main meal. Not bad, right? You can feel very virtuous with this one. No meat, no sugar and only a little bit of sodium. Lots of good shit to help your innards.

Store the rest of the mush for another meal (or share it if it's not just you at home tonight).

STUFFED AVOCADO

So, here's the deal. If a food can be hollowed out, you can stuff it with shit and it'll be delicious. This one is blisstastic and takes only seconds to do with some leftover chicken. A friend served it once with canned tuna, and that was gaggable—but with chicken, it's awesome. I'd like to try it one day with cooked salmon. That would be MEGAtits.

SERVES 1

INGREDIENTS

1 ripe avocado

½ cup (115 g) cooked chicken

1 stalk celery, chopped

¼ cup (40 g) dried fruit

➤ *CHERRIES OR CRANBERRIES ARE THE PRETTIEST*

2 tbsp (30 g) mayonnaise

About 1 tbsp (8 g) candied pecans (page 69), optional

ASSEMBLY AND PREP

Wash the avocado. It's gonna be your dish.

Cut the avocado in half, scoop it out and toss the seed. Cut up the chicken into small pieces and mix with the celery and fruit. Add mayo, and stir gently to mix it all together. Fold in the scooped-out avocado.

SERVE IT UP

Spoon the filling back into the hollowed-out avocado skins. If that grosses you out, then put it on a bed of lettuce or something. Top with some of those candied pecans. You see what I mean?

QUINOA SALAD

This versatile bowl of fiber will soon become a staple of your go-to-work lunchbox—if you like it. Quinoa comes in different colors and swells up more than rice. Cook it long enough that the pods really pop; it tastes amazing when you do that. The cool thing about a simple, grain-based salad like this is that you can supplement it 100 ways from Sunday and it'll taste slightly different every time—and you won't get sick of it. Day one with some grilled veggies and ranch-style dip. Day two, eat out with coworkers. Day three with cheese and crackers. Day four at your fucking desk with no time to leave—just wolf it down and drink your water. Day five, the week is finally over, so add some deli meat and a piece of fresh fruit.

I SERVING AND LEFTOVERS

INGREDIENTS

6–8 mushrooms, washed and sautéed lightly

2 tbsp (30 ml) olive oil

4 tbsp (60 ml) rice vinegar

Pinch each of salt and pepper

2 cups (370 g) cooked quinoa

½ cup (80 g) shelled edamame or snow peas

1 (14-oz [115-g]) can garbanzo beans

1 pack of cherry tomatoes, to slice and add daily

Any other dry spices you like—it's your fucking salad

ASSEMBLY AND PREP

Sauté the mushrooms and set aside to cool. Mix the olive oil, rice vinegar, salt and pepper. Shake or whisk vigorously.

Drizzle the dressing all over the quinoa and stir to blend. Add the edamame and garbanzo beans and store in single-serving containers.

Isn't it pretty? Particularly if you use red quinoa.

SERVE IT UP

Each day you take it to work, slice 2 to 4 tomatoes in half and lay 'em on top. Add something different as a side nibble so it doesn't seem like you're in a fucking rut. Cheese and crackers, jalapeño peppers, pickles, leftover pot roast—your choice, always.

Yes, you read above that you can go out to lunch one day . . . if you want.

SUPER QUICK MINESTRONE FOR ONE

SERVES 1

Minestrone is Italian for fucking good vegetable soup with beans and pasta. My grandma told me that, but she didn't cuss. What? You doubt me? Ha! Score one for me. You can't ask her. Anyway, this is super quick and makes just enough for one person with a single bowl left over. Double or quadruple it if you're expecting an invasion of friends or family. I don't put onions in mine. You can if you want to.

INGREDIENTS

1 (32-oz [905-g]) can/box chicken broth

1 (14-oz [395-g]) bag shredded coleslaw, cabbage-only

1 (12-oz [340-g]) package frozen soup vegetables

1 (15-oz [425-g]) can kidney beans, drained

1 (15-oz [425-g]) can garbanzo beans, drained

1 (28-oz [795-g]) can crushed tomatoes

2 cups (280 g) cooked pasta

⅛ tsp garlic salt, if you like that shit

1 tsp Italian seasoning

Pinch each of salt and pepper

Parmesan cheese to finish it off

ASSEMBLY AND PREP

Get out a big soup pot. Better a big pan now than having to wash two.

Heat the chicken broth to boiling and throw in about 1 cup (340 g) of the cabbage. Cook at a slow boil for 15 to 20 minutes. Add the frozen veggies and bring to a boil again for about 10 minutes. Throw in the beans and tomatoes. Add the cooked pasta and seasonings, and let it simmer for about 10 minutes.

SERVE IT UP

Dish it into a bowl. Sprinkle Parmesan cheese on top. Serve with garlic toast or crackers!

Yes, I know. I said this would serve one . . . that's with one bowl left over. Or, if you're feeling generous, give some to an elderly neighbor who's all alone. Better yet, invite that neighbor over for a nice meal.

SOLO SHRIMP SCAMPI

No need to go out to a fancy schmancy restaurant if you're craving shrimp scampi and it's dinner-for-one tonight. Stop at the store and buy a handful of frozen shrimp if you don't already keep a small bag of 'em in the house—really, you don't? You should. Jus' sayin'. Grab a fresh tomato, some garlic cloves (yuck), some green onions (more yuck), and if you don't normally use cream for anything else, see if you can talk a barista out of an ounce (28 ml) or so. Maybe a generous tip? Now go home and fix this up and feel decadent. Why? Sometimes you just want to be able to slurp spaghetti without anyone judging you and eat shrimp with your fingers all gooped up. The fact that you can then lick this deliciousness off your fingers is a built-in bonus. C'mon, think about it: shrimp, spaghetti, butter and cream, Italian flavors and dripping yumness.

SERVES 1

INGREDIENTS

Enough spaghetti for one serving, about a thumb/pointer finger circle

⅓ lb (150 g) frozen shrimp, pinky finger–sized, tail off

As much fresh garlic as you can handle

1 bunch (1¼ cups [120 g]) green onions, chopped

2 tbsp (30 g) butter

3 tbsp (45 ml) cream

⅛ tsp Italian seasoning—trust me, you need this

Salt, pepper and red pepper flakes to your liking

ASSEMBLE AND COOK

Start cooking your spaghetti. Trim the tails off the shrimp. Mince the garlic and slice the onions. In a frying pan, melt the butter and sauté the shrimp, garlic and onions for 4 to 5 minutes. When the spaghetti is done, drain all but about a teaspoon of the water out of it. Now, put the shit from the frying pan right into the pan with the spaghetti. Add the cream and Italian seasoning, then add salt, pepper and red pepper flakes to taste. Stir quickly and throw it into a bowl.

You're done. Put on your bib and your Luciano Pavarotti playlist.

SERVE IT UP

We covered that part already in the last step above. You weren't reading carefully? Serve a green salad alongside this if you wish. The garlic will keep vampires and lovers at bay for days.

CHICKEN BRUSCHETTA

Orzo is an underrated pasta. It's so easy to cook and mixes well with everything—a regular United Nations kinda thing. I leave the onions out of this when I make it, cuz they don't like me, but you can do whatever you want. This is like toast bruschetta, only better, cuz . . . chicken. Pretend you're on a patio in Sicily, maybe even play some opera music in the background. See? Who says this eating for one can't be a grand fucking adventure every single day?

1 SERVING

INGREDIENTS

½ cup (80 g) cooked orzo pasta

1 chicken breast or thigh, cooked

4–5 mushrooms, sautéed with the chicken

⅛ tsp garlic salt if you like that shit

1 tomato, chopped very small

¼ cup (50 g) red onion, chopped very small

1 tbsp (3 g) fresh basil, chopped eensy teensy

1 tsp olive oil

1 tbsp (15 ml) balsamic vinegar to drizzle

Pinch of salt and pepper

Parmesan cheese to finish it off

ASSEMBLY AND PREP

Dump the pasta, chicken, mushrooms and garlic salt together in a nice big bowl so you can stir it around. Throw on the tomato, onion, basil and olive oil, and then drizzle with the balsamic vinegar. Stir gently, and then sprinkle the salt and pepper along with some Parmesan cheese on top.

SERVE IT UP

Mangia, mangia! Dish it into your favorite bowl. Relax. Oh My Goodness!

ANGEL HAIR RESCUE

SERVES 2

This is so criminally fast that you have to stay on your toes to make sure you don't overcook it. Do all your veggie prep before you put the pasta into the water. AND— this works either cold or hot.

INGREDIENTS

1 red bell pepper, chopped medium

4–5 fresh mushrooms, washed and chopped

Olive oil for sautéing

1 small handful of uncooked angel hair pasta

1 cup (185 g) frozen chopped broccoli

4 tbsp (55 g) butter

½ cup (90 g) grated Parmesan cheese

Salt, pepper and Italian seasoning to taste

ASSEMBLE AND COOK

In a small pan, sauté the pepper and mushrooms in the oil over medium heat for 5 minutes. Boil the angel hair pasta after breaking it into 4-inch (10-cm) strands. Boil the frozen broccoli with it. As soon as the pasta and broccoli are done, drain them and combine in a bowl with the pepper and mushrooms.

To eat it hot, slather that shit with butter, sprinkle liberally with Parmesan cheese, stir and eat. Add seasonings as you prefer.

To serve as a cold side dish, let the pasta/broccoli cool down and then use 1 teaspoon of olive oil instead of butter.

SERVE IT UP

Add a green salad or some cooked meat if you want, and you're good to go.

CRESCENT WONDER

Refrigerator crescent rolls (the name brand or the generic ones) are the universe's gift to a busy day. A little four-pack of them, plus some quick ingredients (really, anything in the shape of the fickle-finger-of-fate will do), and you're good to go. These are very toaster-oven friendly and you can go wild with the different combinations of fillings.

MAKES 3 OR MORE SERVINGS

INGREDIENTS

1 (4-pack) refrigerator crescent rolls

4 tbsp (60 g) BBQ sauce, divided

4 tbsp (60 g) ranch-style dressing, divided

6 tbsp (90 g) chicken breast chunks, cooked

4 tsp (12 g) raisins, divided

ASSEMBLY AND PREP

Preheat the oven or toaster oven to 375°F (190°C). Spread the crescent triangles on a piece of aluminum foil. Barely brush the rolls with the BBQ sauce and ranch. Place some chicken chunks and about 1 teaspoon (3 g) of raisins in the wide end of the triangle. Roll it up with the pointed end sticking up. Pinch to secure it. Repeat for the remaining rolls.

Bake in the oven for the amount of time noted on the package directions.

SERVE IT UP

When they come out of the oven all toasty and browned, dip 'em in the remaining ranch dressing and your hunger disappears.

If you're desperate to feel like you're eating a balanced diet, add a side dish of a lettuce wedge, some rabbit greens or a piece of fruit.

BONUS: I also love these with asparagus and cheese (pictured left).

If you're by yourself and you want to make dessert at the same time, place apple quarters and cinnamon/sugar in two of the crescents and a "main dish" filling in the other two. Voilà! Dinner and dessert at once. Pour a little pancake syrup or sour cream on your plate for dipping the apple crescents.

CREPES—NOT CRAP

This is either breakfast or dessert; it doesn't make any difference. But it's technically only one serving, so here it is in this chapter.

INGREDIENTS

¼ cup (40 g) thawed or fresh strawberries, smashed

8 oz (225 g) vanilla yogurt

½ cup (60 g) just-add-water pancake mix

½ cup (120 ml) room-temperature water

ASSEMBLE AND COOK

Mix the strawberries and yogurt together. Either warm in a saucepan or nuke for 1 minute to get it to room temperature. Mix the pancake batter—it will be thin so you can roll these like crepes.

On a nonstick griddle or frying pan over medium heat, pour the batter into 3 equal pancakes. Fry the pancakes big and round so you can roll 'em like a burrito.

Depending on your version of "medium heat," the pancakes will cook on one side for 2 to 3 minutes until bubbling and bursting air pockets. Then flip 'em over for 1 minute on the second side.

Once you take a pancake out of the pan or griddle, spoon some of the yogurt/berry mix down the middle and fold the two sides over in thirds like a burrito.

SERVE IT UP

Once you have 3 of 'em on your plate, you're ready to eat. Watch the news or catch up on social media. Then go slay dragons for the rest of the day. Or, sleep well if this was your dinner/dessert. Either way, you did good, little bear.

SATISFYING SNACK MIX

I'm always a little disappointed whenever I try to buy a package of snack mix. Invariably it contains something I don't like. Did I mention I'm a bit picky? At 70-plus, I'm entitled to my opinion. I actually like to have two kinds of snack mix on hand. One is a combo of sweet and nutty (like me, of course) and works perfectly to sneak into the movie theatre. The other is a bit more appetizer-ish and works well when I just need a little something to tide me over until the next meal. It's really just a mix-and-match kinda thing, so pick what you like. Want coconut? Add it. I don't give a flying fart. Just warn me ahead of time cuz I don't like it.

MAKES ABOUT 5 CUPS (600 G)

INGREDIENTS—SWEET AND NUTTY

1 (8-oz [225-g]) package walnut pieces

1 (8-oz [225-g]) package pecan pieces

1 cup (150 g) raisins

1 cup (150 g) dried cranberries

½ cup (80 g) dried pineapple

1 (42-oz [1.2-kg]) package plain M&Ms

INGREDIENTS—APPETIZER

1 cup (20 g) Chex cereal

1 cup (70 g) small skinny pretzels

1 cup (110 g) salted cashews, whole or pieces

½ cup (55 g) salted peanuts

½ cup (115 g) jerky, cut into tiny bits

½ cup (70 g) sunflower seeds

ASSEMBLY AND PREP

Really, just pour the shit into a big zip-top bag or a big-ass bowl, stir or shake it up and then separate it into smaller bags or airtight containers for snackage.

SERVE IT UP

Open the bag or container, put your grubby mitt in and grab a handful. Then pop it in your mouth. DONE! Oh, and have hand wipes available cuz this shit is gonna mess with you, salt or sugar.

MY FAVORITE FRUITY ICE CUBES

I'm an ice-cream fanatic—and a fruit freak—and I really shouldn't eat a whole bunch of either, so this is one way I trick myself into thinking I had a treat when truthfully I was a bit kinder to my pancreas. My favorite combo so far has been frozen mango pieces with strawberries and pineapple juice. Pick your favorites, though. Apple juice works well with anything, and orange juice with bananas and strawberries is orgasmic.

MAKES AT LEAST 1 TRAY

INGREDIENTS

1 cup (165 g) frozen mango cubes

1 cup (150 g) fresh or frozen strawberries

½ cup (120 ml) pineapple juice

1 (8-oz [225-g]) container vanilla yogurt

ASSEMBLY AND PREP

Take about a cup of each fruit out to thaw about an hour before you start. You won't use the whole bag, so there will be plenty left over to go in the other recipes in this book.

Pour the juice in the blender first, followed by the yogurt. Add the almost-thawed fruit last. Blend super well, leaving a few chunks.

Now, pour it into an ice-cube tray and refreeze.

SERVE IT UP

Today's self-defrosting refrigerators take the moisture out of everything, so once these are frozen, dump them into a zip-top bag and put them back into the freezer.

NOTE: There are so many ways to eat these, but my favorite is just to stand at the sink and eat one like a popsicle. Then I turn on the faucet and wash my hands. Bam, back to work without a huge sugar rush.

SOUP'S ON

Soup is one of the most forgiving food combos ever invented. I can just picture some cave people huddled out of the rain in a storm, throwing in some green weeds, some leftover jerky, some rainwater, maybe some tree bark and some goat's milk in a desperate attempt to stretch what little food they had, fill their bellies and keep warm by the fire.

Yeah, that was a stretch, but just go with me, will ya? I'm a storyteller and an actress, and you want drama, right? In your own home cave, throw together shit that you like or follow these recipes, and stay out of the rain or snow or whatever-the-fuck Mom Nature throws your way. Ladle up!

LOADED BAKED POTATO SOUP

Who'da thunk that potato soup could be so fuckin' yummy. AND easy when you use potatoes that somebody else already prepped. I guess this is the hot version of my genius FAST as FUCK potato salad, right? (See page 62.) With shit you've already got in your cupboard or freezer, you can turn a bad-weather day into sunshine at the table.

SERVES 8-10

INGREDIENTS

1 (30-oz [850-g]) bag frozen hash browns (cubes or shredded)

OR 8-10 MEDIUM POTATOES CUT SMALL, BOILED 'TIL DONE AND THEN SMASHED. REALLY? YOU WANNA DO ALL THAT WORK? KNOCK YOURSELF OUT!

1 (28-oz [800-ml]) can/box chicken broth

1 (10-oz [285-g]) can cream of chicken/celery soup

2 tbsp (10 g) dried minced onion or 1 tsp onion powder

½ tsp ground black pepper

8 oz (225 g) cream cheese, softened

1 tbsp (15 ml) Worcestershire sauce

½ cup (115 g) or more cubed ham

2 cups (240 g) shredded cheddar cheese, divided in thirds

OPTIONAL INGREDIENTS FOR TOPPING

¼ cup (30 g) crispy bacon bits

¼ cup (15 g) freshly sliced green onions

ASSEMBLY AND PREP

Mix the frozen hash browns (no need to thaw), chicken broth, the can of creamed soup, minced onion and pepper in a slow cooker. Cook on low for 5 hours.

After you get home, remove the lid and stir in the cream cheese and Worcestershire sauce. Stir thoroughly so the cream cheese spreads evenly. Close the lid and cook for another 30 minutes. Stir thoroughly one more time.

JUST before serving, mix in the ham cubes and a third of the cheddar cheese.

SERVE IT UP

Serve with bacon, green onions and the remaining cheddar on top. Add a little side salad or some steamed veggies, and everybody's happy. Food pyramid, ya know?

CHICKEN TACO SOUP

Who says you can't have tacos and soup in one? Nobody! This is as good as you'll get in any Mexican restaurant in any country in the world. And—Mexican food, jus' sayin'. What's not to love? Because you have to do this in two steps of about 2 hours each, it's best to do it on a day when you're not at work. Still, it's FAST as FUCK for prep, and that's what counts the most.

SERVES 6-8

INGREDIENTS

1 onion, chopped small

1 (16-oz [455-g]) can pinto beans

1 (15-oz [425-g]) can black beans

1 (15-oz [425-g]) can whole-kernel corn, drained

1 (8-oz [225-g]) can tomato sauce

1 (12-oz [355-ml]) can or bottle of beer

1 (28-oz [795-g]) can diced tomatoes

1 (1¼-oz [35-g]) package taco seasoning

3 whole skinless, boneless chicken breasts

OPTIONAL INGREDIENTS FOR TOPPING/SERVING

Sliced green onions

Shredded cheddar cheese or Mexican-blend cheese

Sour cream

Crushed tortilla chips

Jalapeño peppers

Your favorite hot sauce

ASSEMBLY AND PREP

Place the onion, pinto beans, black beans, corn, tomato sauce, beer and diced tomatoes in a slow cooker. Add the taco seasoning and stir to blend. Lay the chicken breasts on top of the mixture, pressing down slightly until just covered by the other ingredients. Set the slow cooker for low heat, cover and cook for 5 hours.

Remove the chicken breasts from the soup and allow to cool long enough to be handled. Pull the chicken breasts apart and cut so that no piece is too big to fit on a spoon. Stir the shredded/cut chicken back into the soup, and continue cooking for 2 hours.

SERVE IT UP

Serve in big bowls alongside small bowls of the optional toppings and hot sauces. OMFG, watch your guests go to town.

As a bonus, warm up some corn or flour tortillas and have 'em ready on the table.

If you need to stretch this meal, serve a big green salad with it.

BROCCOLI CHEESE RAPTURE (SOUP)

SERVES 4–6

Yes, it's very legal to use prepared foods to whip up a quick pot of soup. And with some clever adaptations, you can't tell this from the soup-they-buy-in-a-bag that is served in swanky restaurants. Rapture, baby, and it takes less than 10 minutes to prepare.

INGREDIENTS

1 (10-oz [250-g]) bag frozen broccoli

1 (10-oz [285-g]) can low-salt cream of celery soup

1½ soup cans of milk

4 oz (115 g) shredded cheddar cheese

4 oz (115 g) shredded Colby/Jack cheese mix

2 oz (55 g) cream cheese
NOT THE WHIPPED KIND

½ tsp Worcestershire sauce

ASSEMBLY AND PREP

Might as well start out with a 2-quart (2-L) pan, cuz why dirty two of 'em?

Steam the broccoli in ¾ cup (180 ml) of boiling water 'til it's fork tender, about 6 minutes. Drain the water out, and then add the soup and the milk. Turn the heat to medium-low and stir it all together.

After 5 to 7 minutes, add the shredded cheeses and cream cheese, and stir until it's melted evenly. While stirring the melted cheese, add the Worcestershire sauce. Add a little more milk if it looks too thick and goopy.

SERVE IT UP

Pour right into your favorite bowl and experience rapture!

BLACK-EYED PEAS—SOUTHERN STYLE

Cornbread and black-eyed peas are widely regarded as the sure-fire recipe for good luck if consumed on New Year's Day. It's decidedly an American thing, and decidedly Southern, but so frickin' delicious that even the Yanks have been known to cook up a fine pot o' peas. Ay yup! Cornbread, don't forget to fix a batch of cornbread or the luck thing won't happen. Don't fuck with the luck.

SERVES 6

INGREDIENTS

4–5 slices of bacon or leftover ham

1 fist-sized onion, chopped

2 carrots, chopped

1 stalk celery, chopped

6 cups (1.4 L) chicken broth

½ tsp garlic salt

½ tsp regular salt

¼ tsp black pepper

4 cups (805 g) fresh or frozen black-eyed peas

TOPPINGS
Sliced tomatoes

Your favorite hot sauce

ASSEMBLE AND COOK

In a big-ass soup pan, cook the bacon until crisp. Set aside to drain.

Cook the onion, carrots and celery in the bacon drippings until tender, maybe 5 to 6 minutes. Add the broth, salts, pepper and peas. Bring to a rolling boil, and skim the top if it looks yucky.

Lower the heat to simmer and cook 40 to 50 minutes, or until the peas are as tender as you prefer. Some like 'em hard, some like 'em soft—you pick.

Stir every now and then, tasting to adjust the seasonings. Just before serving, crumble the bacon, slice some tomatoes, grab some hot sauce— oh, and I hope you remembered the cornbread.

SERVE IT UP
Dish the cooked peas into bowls, top with the bacon and go to town. Good luck follows you all year.

GRANNY'S 100% VEGGIE SOUP

SERVES 8-10

If you're veggie, or you are expecting guests who are, this is soooo easy and so yummy. Adding a can of lentils, some brown rice or some cooked barley bumps it up a notch or two, providing just the weight you need to make this satisfying as fuck.

INGREDIENTS

2 qts (2 L) veggie stock

NOT BROTH

1 stalk celery, sliced very thin, even the leaves

4–6 carrots, sliced very thin

1 large onion, chopped into small pieces

1 (12- to 14-oz [340- to 395-g]) bag frozen green beans, thawed to room temp

1 (12- to 14-oz [340- to 395-g]) bag frozen broccoli cuts, thawed to room temp

1 (12- to 14-oz [340- to 395-g] bag whole-kernel corn, thawed to room temp

1 (28-oz [795-g]) can crushed tomatoes

1 (16-oz [455-g]) can lentils, like Progresso

2 cups (315 g) cooked brown rice

OPTIONAL INGREDIENTS FOR THICKENING

2 cups (370 g) cooked barley instead of the rice, if you prefer

1 cup (325 g) instant mashed potatoes to thicken, if you wish

ASSEMBLY AND PREP

In a big-ass pan on top of the stove, bring the 2 jugs of broth to a boil.

Throw the celery, carrots and onion in the broth. When they're just about done to chewable consistency, maybe 10 minutes, throw in all the thawed veggie shit. Once that starts to bubble around the edges, throw in the tomatoes and lentils. Once that mess starts to get warm, add in the brown rice or barley to thicken.

Let it simmer on the burner, cover on the pan, for about 30 minutes.

SERVE IT UP

This can cook slowly for 3 to 4 hours and will taste better each time you reheat it.

BUT don't boil it forever or it'll just be mush.

TIP: If you want to destroy the veggie vibe, substitute beef broth, some cooked meat and there ya go.

CREAMLESS CREAMY SOUP BASE

Okay, so this isn't technically a fully prepared soup recipe, but, hey, just keep reading, okay? My gramma absolutely hated prepared foods. She swore she could make better shit than would ever be found in a can or a fucking frozen dinner (we called 'em TV dinners back then). In truth, she was absolutely justified in her indignation. Her soup base would turn garden veggies or cheap stew meat into heaven-in-a-bowl in about 30 minutes. I still keep an airtight container of this in the cupboard at all times in case inspiration hits. It's for all of you who really don't trust the seasonings, spices or preservatives in prepared cream-of-anything soup. Yes, it takes a little more time than opening a can (which is perfectly justified in this millennium), so it's not technically FAST as FUCK, but it's time-tested and Granny proven, so there. It's full-on Suzy Homemaker, back-to-nature Mama. And, truth be told, when you want soup fast and you're out of canned cream soups, this will turn out to be just the FAST as FUCK you need.

Since you probably have to buy these ingredients in more quantity than you need for a single batch of soup base, double or triple it when you mix it all up so that the dry ingredients don't go to waste. As long as you keep it in separate portions of 1¼ cups (300 ml) each in airtight containers, you're good for up to a year.

MAKES 1 BATCH, BUT SERIOUSLY, KNOCK YOURSELF OUT

· ·

INGREDIENTS FOR A SINGLE BATCH

1 cup (110 g) nonfat dry milk powder

2 tbsp (20 g) cornstarch

2 tbsp (12 g) bouillon powder

BEEF, CHICKEN OR VEGGIE

1 tbsp (8 g) flour

EVEN RICE FLOUR WORKS FOR THE GF VERSION

1 tbsp (15 g) salt

1 tbsp (8 g) black pepper

½ tsp onion powder

½ tsp thyme

½ tsp basil

¼ tsp oregano

¼ tsp garlic powder

ASSEMBLY AND PREP

In a soup pot, combine all the ingredients. Add 2 cups (475 ml) of water to the dry mix and warm up on medium heat until it thickens, about 4 to 6 minutes, stirring constantly. It's the cornstarch and flour that make it robust, but it will burn and clump if you don't stir constantly.

Once it's heated and creamy, add in ½ to ¾ cup of your favorite ingredient that's been chopped up VERY small (you want cream of broccoli, or zucchini, or cauliflower?). Now cover, turn the heat to low and cook until that ingredient is fork tender, probably 20 to 30 minutes. Stir frequently to keep from sticking, clumping or getting a slimy top coat. Remember this is the soup base, not the soup. You still have to put shit in it—anything from veggies to meat to a combo. It's a creamy soup base, not a broth base.

For thicker, more hearty soup, add more chopped ingredients and stir diligently.

SERVE IT UP
Right? I told you! Heaven-in-a-bowl, just like Gramma made in the 1950s.

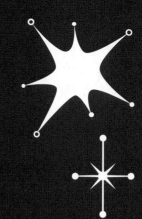

SWEET TOOTH

NOOOOOOOOOOOOWWWW we're talking. Sweet shit—my downfall. Why do you think I weigh over 200 pounds? But, in small doses, or fixed for company or a potluck, or eaten in moderation—it's all good. Fruit is full of natural sugar, so fill your gob with that whenever you can. Add it to other ingredients for lots of interesting texture.

The chocolate berry parfait dessert (see page 152) was a big experiment and, to date, is my favorite recipe to prepare for friends. There's a surprise in every bite. I'm big on enjoying my food, not just putting it into my piehole knowing it'll come out another hole after a journey through my innards.

Try them all and lemme know which one is the biggest hit with you or your fam or friends.

CHOCOLATE BERRY PARFAIT DESSERT

In my world, chocolate is its own food group. Melted or frozen, liquid or solid, mixed in or poured over—it rocks. So, with that for starters, how 'bout we add fresh fruit and some cake? Hold on to the counter, Mama, we're taking a ride on the Dessert Express to Heaven. Pay attention to the flow of this recipe. Do your prep ahead of time so you can layer easily once the pudding is just about set.

INGREDIENTS

2 cups (300 g) fresh strawberries, washed, sliced and packed firmly into a measuring cup

USE FROZEN STRAWBERRIES IF FRESH ARE NOT IN SEASON (THAW BEFORE ASSEMBLING THE PARFAIT)

1–2 cups (140–280 g) fresh blueberries, washed and de-stemmed

2 tbsp (25 g) granulated sugar, optional

Fresh or stale chocolate cupcakes or cake

1 (6-oz [170-g]) package instant chocolate pudding

Milk sufficient to make pudding as directed

Chocolate syrup for finishing

OPTIONAL

Whipped cream and/or whole strawberries for topping/garnish

PREP

Combine the berries in a bowl and sprinkle lightly with the sugar (go easy on your pancreas). Put a big spoon in that bowl so you're ready to move fast. Break the cupcakes or cake into walnut-sized nuggets, and set aside in a separate bowl.

GET READY TO ROCK AND ROLL

Set out 4 bowls or wide-mouth drinking glasses (clear is best so you can see how pretty it is).

TA DA

Mix the pudding according to directions on the package. DO NOT OVERMIX or you're in deep shit, cuz you won't be able to spoon it into the bowls.

ASSEMBLE

When the pudding is just about set, start layering in the dishes or glasses

1. PUDDING
2. FRUIT
3. CAKE
4. PUDDING
5. FRUIT
6. CAKE
7. LAST DOLLOP of PUDDING if there's any left

Put it in the fridge or freezer 'til serving time, but don't freeze.

SERVE IT UP FANCY

Top with the chocolate syrup, and (if you like) whipped cream and a fresh whole strawberry, stem and leaves still included.

MEGA-NUT CHOCO BROWNIES

I'm such a pushover for chocolate. This is my current version of something I first started messing with in the early 1980s in order to combine my love for cakey brownies with my desire for more chocolatey goo in every bite. Oh, and nuts—gotta have nuts. Don't fuckin' forget the nuts. (Sh-h-h-h, the peanut butter is a secret.) Ordinarily, I don't like to combine chocolate and peanut butter—I know, I'm defective—but this is my redemption right here.

MAKES 12

INGREDIENTS

1 box double-chocolate brownie mix

YOU'LL NEED OIL, WATER AND EGGS TO MAKE THE BROWNIES

¼ cup (30 g) pecans, smashed up

½ cup (30 g) walnuts, smashed up

½ cup (90 g) semi-sweet chocolate chips

Some peanut butter to make surprise pockets

ASSEMBLY AND PREP

Preheat the oven to 350°F (177°C). Grease up a 9 x 13–inch (23 x 33–cm) baking dish.

Mix the brownies according to the package directions for cakey brownies (oil, water, eggs, etc.). Add the nuts and chocolate chips, fuck yeah! Bake for 25 to 30 minutes, and then do the toothpick test.

SERVE IT UP

As soon as you take the pan out of the oven, poke a mess of holes in the top with a meat fork. Spread a thin layer of peanut butter across the top of the brownies, and let it sink into the holes. If you can still see peanut butter, poke more holes so it seeps into the top. Let 'em cool before you try to cut 'em.

The trick here is to try to make the peanut butter a stealthy surprise.

CHOCOLATE CHERRY WALNUT COOKIES

How 'bout a fruit spin on the classic chocolate chip cookie? Yeah, cherries. You read that right. You've eaten chocolate-covered cherries, right? And chocolate-covered walnuts, too, I bet? Well, this is the best of both those worlds in a cookie.

DRY INGREDIENTS

2¼ cups (280 g) unsifted flour

1 tsp baking soda

½ tsp salt

CREAMY INGREDIENTS

1 cup (2 sticks [230 g]) butter, softened

¾ cup (110 g) brown sugar

¾ cup (145 g) sugar

3 tsp (15 ml) vanilla extract

YES, THAT MUCH

2 large eggs

THE GOOD SHIT AT THE END

2 cups (360 g) dark chocolate chips

1 cup (150 g) dried sour cherries

1 cup (115 g) walnuts, roughly chopped

ASSEMBLY AND PREP

Mix together the dry ingredients and set aside.

In a separate bowl, mix the butter and sugars together 'til creamy. Add the vanilla. Add the eggs one at a time, and beat by hand until well mixed into the butter/sugar mixture. Now, gradually blend the dry ingredients into the creamed ingredients. Then add the chocolate chips, cherries and nuts. This will be very stiff dough. You'll need muscles to blend it.

Heat your oven to 375°F (190°C). Scoop up about a teaspoonful of dough at a time and drop it onto an ungreased cookie sheet. Bake for 12 to 15 minutes depending on your preferred state of crispy/gooey.

SERVE 'EM UP

Glass of cold milk or cup of coffee, and you're good to go.

> **NOTE:** Heat your oven to 385°F (196°C) if you like your cookies super crispy. Something magical happens when you expose sugar and butter to high heat. Chemistry. No, seriously. Caramelization adds to the flavor . . . if you like it that way.

MAMA'S FAMOUS APPLE CAKE

Easier than apple pie and even more satisfying. Adding nuts, raisins and dried cranberries make this festive as fuck . . . any time of year. Yum City.

● ●

MAIN INGREDIENTS

4 eggs

2 cups (385 g) sugar

1 cup (235 ml) oil

2 cups (250 g) flour

6 apples, thinly sliced (about 3 cups [540 g] or so)

½ tsp salt

4 tsp (15 g) baking powder

4 tsp (10 g) cinnamon

2 tsp (10 ml) vanilla extract

1 cup (115 g) chopped walnuts

¼ cup (40 g) raisins

¼ cup (40 g) dried cranberries

INGREDIENTS FOR TOPPING

2 tbsp (25 g) sugar

1 tsp cinnamon

ASSEMBLY AND PREP

Preheat the oven to 350°F (177°C). Grease up a 9 x 13–inch (23 x 33–cm) baking dish.

In a big-ass bowl, mix all of the main ingredients together with a heavy spatula or sturdy wooden spoon. DON'T USE A MIXER. You'll overmix it.

Press/pour that clumpy mess into the baking dish. Now mix the topping ingredients together in a small bowl and spread evenly over the top. Bake uncovered for maybe 50 to 60 minutes, giving it the clean-knife test at 40 minutes.

SERVE IT UP

Cut it into squares right in the pan, and watch it disappear. That shit won't last, I promise.

SUPER FAST PUMPKIN BUNDT

Sometimes you wanna show off your "from scratch" skills, even though you don't have a whole day to fuck around in the kitchen. This cake is so easy it almost makes itself. Pumpkin, what can I say? It's so versatile it oughta be sold at McD's.

DRY INGREDIENTS

2 cups (385 g) sugar

2 cups (250 g) flour

2 tsp (9 g) baking soda

NOT BAKING POWDER, DUH

2 tsp (5 g) cinnamon

½ tsp pumpkin pie spice

Pinch of salt

MOIST INGREDIENTS

1 (15-oz [425-g]) can pumpkin

3 extra-large or 4 large eggs, beaten

1 cup (235 ml) oil

¼ tsp vanilla extract

ASSEMBLY AND PREP

Preheat the oven to 300°F (150°C). Grease and flour a bundt pan.

Mix the dry ingredients by hand in a small bowl. Mix the moist ingredients by hand in a big bowl. Fold the dry shit into the moist shit slowly so you don't make a mess. DON'T overmix or use a mixer. Use a hefty spoon or spatula. Pour it into the bundt pan and bake for an hour.

If you start this before you start dinner, you can have dessert with ice cream by the time the plates are cleared from dinner. Oh, and you'll be the family god or goddess. But don't do it every day or they'll start to take you for granted.

SERVE IT UP

We just went over that. Slice, put in a bowl, top with vanilla ice cream. DONE!

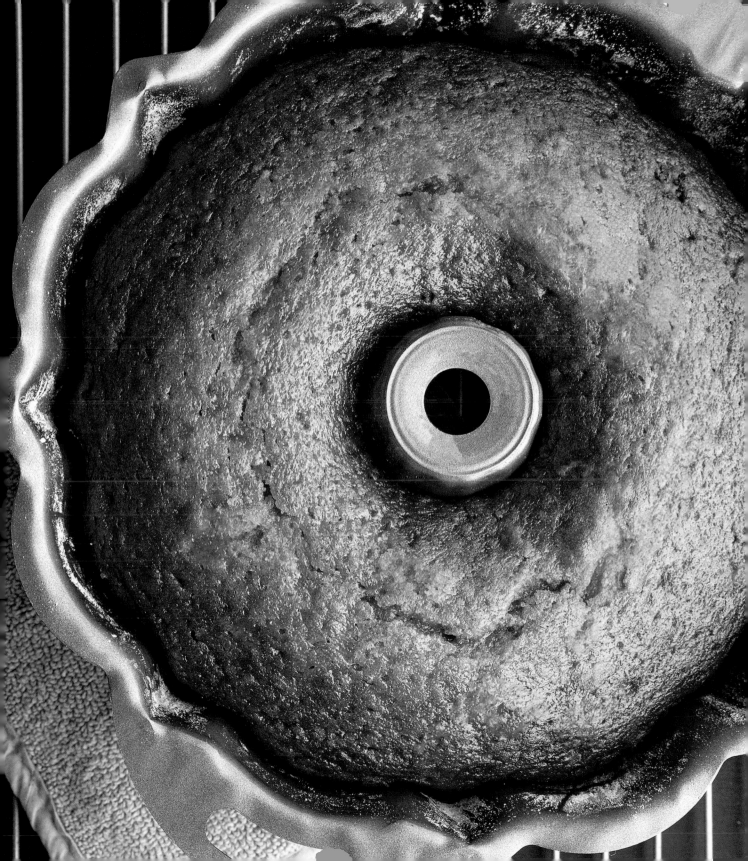

BANANA RAISIN BONANZA

Watching your sugar? I've got just the thing—so satisfying and so fucking simple. Now, you know, bananas are like avocados when it comes to ripeness . . . or not. Tomorrow, tomorrow, tomorrow, too late. This time you're in luck. Too-late bananas are perfect. Sometimes you can even find them super cheap in the bargain aisle of the produce section of your market. Once a month or so, I hang out for a morning of brainstorming with a bunch of creative women, and 90 percent of them are picking at kale and calling it food. I can't hang with that, so I brought these to share one month, and they actually ate them. SCORE!

SERVES 6-8

INGREDIENTS

3 ripe bananas

⅓ cup (80 g) applesauce

2 cups (320 g) quick-cooking oats

¼ cup (60 ml) milk

½ cup (75 g) raisins

1 tsp vanilla extract

1 tsp cinnamon

ASSEMBLY AND PREP

Preheat the oven to 350°F (177°C). Grease up a 9 x 9–inch (23 x 23–cm) baking dish. Smash the bananas 'til they're a snotty mess. Put them and the rest of the shit into a bowl, and mix it up with a solid spatula. Pour the thick mess into the baking dish. Bake for 15 to 20 minutes.

SERVE IT UP

Let these cool for 15 to 20 minutes so you don't burn your mouth devouring their amazing non-sugary goodness.

HOT PINEAPPLE PERFECTION

You know I'm a freak for pineapple, right? It goes in everything but scrambled eggs. Nothing could be easier than this. It's sort of bread pudding and sort of cheesecake. It's definitely orgasmic and delicious. I mean, really—hot and pineapple. What can I say?

MAKES 1 CAKE, NO, REALLY, TEE HEE

INGREDIENTS

1 stick (½ cup [115 g]) of butter, room temperature

1 cup (190 g) sugar

4 eggs

1 (20-oz [565-g]) can crushed pineapple, drained

6 slices of white bread, crusts removed, cut into cubes

4 oz (115 g) package of cream cheese, softened, cubed

ASSEMBLY AND PREP

Preheat the oven to 350°F (177°C). Grease and flour a 9 x 13–inch (23 x 33–cm) casserole pan.

Cream the butter and sugar together. Add the eggs, and mix by hand until blended. Stir in the pineapple. Fold in the bread cubes. Ooze that amazing shit into the casserole dish. Top randomly with cream cheese cubes.

Bake for 45 minutes.

SERVE IT UP

Let cool for 15 minutes. Slice and serve. BOING!

REFRIGERATOR LEMON PIE

OMG. Nothing will transport me back to my gramma's kitchen faster than lemon bars—I could never replicate them, no matter how hard I tried, but this quick refrigerator lemon pie comes pretty fucking close. The taste is the same, even if it's not her fairy-light bar pastry. Before I had a mini food processor, I put the pecans in a plastic zip-top bag and beat the shit out of them with a hammer.

SERVES 6

CRUST

¼ cup (30 g) pecans, ground small

1 already-prepared graham-cracker pie crust, thawed

2 tbsp (30 ml) melted butter

DON'T USE MARGARINE

FILLING

1 (14-oz [395-g]) can sweetened condensed milk

2 beaten egg yolks at room temperature

⅓ cup (80 ml) lemon juice

ASSEMBLY AND PREP—THE CRUST

Press the smashed pecans into the graham cracker crust once it thaws. Drizzle the melted butter evenly over the nuts/crust.

ASSEMBLY AND PREP—THE FILLING

Use a whisk or an electric mixer to combine the milk, beaten egg yolks and lemon juice. Beat well until it starts to thicken. Pour into the pie crust and let it cool in the fridge.

Now, try to not devour it in one day.

SERVE IT UP

If you're feeling particularly decadent, smash up some more pecans and sprinkle on top.

ACKNOWLEDGMENTS

Ideas come at me like bird shit—when I least expect them and when I'm paying attention to something else. This one showed up at VidCon, the clusterfuck of swarming, screaming prepubescent females held in early June in Anaheim, California. I escaped the madness to attend a panel presentation by successful digital creators who cooked. Donal Skehan was ladling out advice about his upload schedule: complicated recipes on the weekends, when people had more time, and quick-to-fix recipes mid-week when time was precious. WOW. I translated that wisdom nugget in a nanosecond to FAST as FUCK—yeah, that was my brand all right. I was fired up right away and it took only a couple weeks to crank out the first video. Holy fucknuts! My fried rice video went million-view viral in 27 days on YouTube.

Within a week of hitting a million, the smart folks at Page Street Publishing in my childhood home state of Massachusetts (same county that I was raised in, matter of fact), asked if I would and could do a cookbook in 90 days. Fuck yeah! Bay State Savvy—let's get this shit done! Go Sox! Go Pats! Go Celtics! Bruins, meh.

My fans, my creator colleagues, my friends and my sweet man all formed a supportive cheering squad while I buried myself testing out shit, filming shit and writing up recipes. They're all the bomb. Here's some alphabet soup of the peeps who stuck it out with me: JVB, RK, VC, JK, CG. Oh, and my gramma, EBF, was the best baker on the planet. My mom MJFM was a really good cook, too, and she taught me the secret of a well-stocked pantry at an early age. Thanks everybody.

And thank you for buying this, reading it, cooking good shit and telling your friends.

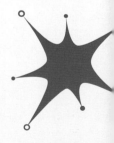

ABOUT THE AUTHOR

Granny PottyMouth is 85% Peggy Glenn with a 15% overlay of her wild and crazy imagination—the part of her that NEVER grew UP, NEVER grew OLD, but did gain wisdom with each experience. Every milestone birthday after 50 was more and more of a permission slip to do whatever-the-fuck she wanted to do as long as she didn't hurt anyone or herself—well, other than aches, pains and road rash from, you know, that time she tried to breakdance while frying an egg on the sidewalk when the temperature reached 121° F (49° C) in Los Angeles. What? You didn't catch the video of that? Gotta stay on top of her shit, ya know.

She currently lives on the outskirts of the Los Angeles city limits so that she can grab any acting opportunity that comes her way without fighting too much traffic, but her heart and spirit will always be 70 miles south in Huntington Beach, California, where everything feels right when the sun sets behind Catalina Island. Oh, and she travels a lot to listen to good music and visit good friends.

Yes, she loves to cook. Yes, she gives advice at the drop of a hat. Yes, she'll correct your fucking pronoun use when you use I/me incorrectly or put apostrophes where they don't belong. Yes, she's a softie in the middle—a full-on marshmallow. But she doesn't like marshmallows. She likes pineapple. And Maui. Don't forget that.

INDEX